D0382740

Tea & Treats

Tea & Treats

perfect pairings for brews and bakes

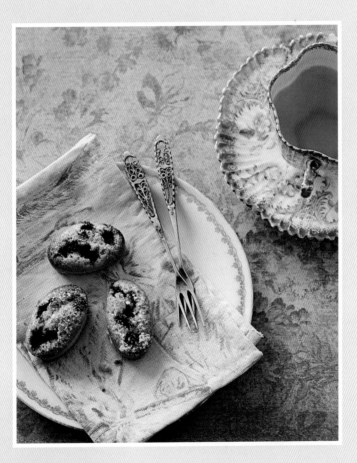

Liz Franklin
photography by Isobel Wield

LONDON • NEW YORK

Senior Designer Sonya Nathoo
Commissioning Editors
Céline Hughes and Stephanie Milner
Head of Production Patricia Harrington
Art Director Leslie Harrington
Editorial Director Julia Charles

Prop Stylist Polly Webb-Wilson
Food Stylist Lizzie Harris
Copy Editor Laura Gladwin
Indexer Hilary Bird

First published in 2014 by
Ryland Peters & Small
20–21 Jockey's Fields,
London WC1R 4BW
and
519 Broadway, 5th Floor,
New York NY 10012

www.rylandpeters.com

10 9 8 7 6 5 4 3 2 1

Text © Liz Franklin 2014
Design and photographs
© Ryland Peters & Small 2014

ISBN: 978-1-84975-497-2   *5440 6318* *07/14*

Printed and bound in China

A CIP record for this book is available from
the British Library.

US Library of Congress Cataloging-in-Publication
Data has been applied for.

Notes
• All spoon measurements are level unless
otherwise specified.
• All eggs are medium (UK) or large (US),
unless otherwise specified. Uncooked or partially
cooked eggs should not be served to the very old,
frail, young children, pregnant women or those
with compromised immune systems.
• When a recipe calls for the grated zest of citrus
fruit, buy unwaxed fruit and wash well before using.
If you can only find treated fruit, scrub well in
warm soapy water before using.
• Ovens should be preheated to the specified
temperatures. We recommend using an oven
thermometer. If using a fan-assisted oven, adjust
temperatures according to the manufacturer's
instructions.

CONTENTS

INTRODUCTION

I grew up in North Yorkshire, where tea was tea. At my house, it was made with loose leaves in a teapot and 'mashed' (brewed) until it was dark and robustly flavoured. It was served with a smidgen of milk, nothing else. It was wet and warm and sometimes so strong you could almost stand a spoon up in it, the sort of tea that builders are notoriously supposed to thrive on, but that was how it was then – back in the days when pasta meant spaghetti hoops in a tin and olive oil came from the chemist!

As I began to discover the myriad teas available, I came to appreciate that different teas have unique characteristics and flavours, and can be suited to a wide array of occasions. A cup of tea can help

perk us up when we're flagging a little, calm us down when we're restless, lift us when we're feeling low, help us celebrate with friends and soothe us when we feel under the weather. Quality teas can bring out the best in the food we choose to eat alongside our chosen cuppa, just as the right fine wine can enhance a plate of food.

Learning to appreciate that a first flush is nothing to do with a visit to the bathroom, that orange pekoe doesn't actually taste of orange, and that plucking isn't only for the eyebrows, has been one of the most enjoyable experiences I have had over the years. Matching the multitude of stunning teas that are now available to us with lovely homemade sweet treats has been an absolute delight. I hope you will enjoy the recipes and revel in new discoveries just as much as I have.

After water, tea is the most widely consumed drink in the world, yet it is often thought of as being a character-istically British drink. It is true that tea has been sipped and slurped all over Britain for several centuries, but to trace the real origins of tea, we have to travel back around 5,000 years to China.

Legend would have it that while travelling one day Emperor Shen Nung was sitting beneath a tree waiting for his servant to boil some drinking water. A light breeze stirred, and a number of leaves from the tree blew into the water. The Emperor is credited with being the father of Chinese medicine and an expert in pharmacology, so the newly created infusion naturally aroused his curiosity and he drank it. The tree in question was *Camellia sinensis* – the evergreen plant whose leaves we now cultivate to produce tea – and the brew was the first cup of tea.

Although we have no real proof of this story, tea containers and related paraphernalia were found in ancient tombs dating back to 206 BC and the Han dynasty, although it was several hundred years later, during the the Tang dynasty, that tea found its place as the national drink of China.

By the 8th century, touring Japanese Buddhist monks had introduced tea to Japan from China and the Chinese were trading tea with Tibet along the famous 5,000 km Ancient Tea Horse Road. Business soon spread further into Asia and beyond.

Fast forward a few hundred years to the late 16th century, and tea had reached European shores. Portuguese traders and missionaries travelling in the Far East are thought to have brought tea back to their own countries, but it was the Dutch who first began shipping tea to Holland, where it became a fashionable drink. From there, tea drinking spread to other western European countries, although high production and transportation costs meant that tea remained a drink available only to the wealthy population.

In 1662 in England, the marriage of Catherine of Braganza (a Portuguese princess and tea enthusiast) to King Charles II made tea fashionable in the Royal Court, and from there it continued to gather a following among aristocracy. As tea began to reach less affluent sections of the population, much mystery, mayhem and very likely the odd murder or two ensued. The costliness of tea was partly down to huge government-imposed taxes, so criminal gangs resorted to smuggling and often adulteration of the leaves in order to keep up with demand for supplies for the working classes.

Ironically, although we now know that tea is a healthy drink, it was suspected at the time that tea drinking could lead to infirmity and depression and was discouraged among those who had to earn their living. However, it soon became accepted that tea was a more suitable drink than alcohol when it came to wetting the whistle of the working classes.

Eventually, the government lowered the taxes and they were finally lifted altogether in 1861. And so began the rise and rise of tea drinking in Great Britain.

ALL ABOUT TEA

We are increasingly discovering the health benefits and enjoyment to be had from drinking tea. However, the differences between types of teas can be quite confusing at first, so I have outlined the main types of tea here. Some of the recipes include teas that aren't technically teas at all, in the strictest sense of the word, in that they are not made from the leaves of *Camellia sinensis*; they are the caffeine-free infusions of various herbs and spices, often referred to as 'tisanes'.

TYPES OF TEA

There are six main types of tea, but within these types there are a whole host of varieties. Once you get to grips with the characteristics and flavours of the different types, you will find that an exciting new adventure has begun.

BLACK TEA

Usually strong and earthy, black teas are fully oxidized and are produced using one of two methods. In the orthodox method, the fresh tea leaves are withered for several hours and then rolled, which releases oils that coat the surface of the still-green leaves. The leaves are left until fully oxidized and then fired to prevent them from rotting. The alternative method is a mechanical process known as CTC (crush, tear, curl) and experts believe that on the whole, teas produced using this method are of a lower grade.

Black tea is used as the base of many popular flavoured teas. Earl Grey is a blend of black tea infused with oil from the bergamot orange. English and Irish breakfast teas are based on the leaves of full-bodied black teas and India's favourite Masala Chai is a sweet and aromatic blend of black tea, milk and spices that is gaining in popularity around the world now. Lapsang Souchong, Assam, Darjeeling, Ceylon and Keemun are all well known varieties of black tea.

GREEN TEA

Unlike black teas, green teas do not go through any form of oxidization (the chemical changes that happen after exposure to air). They can be first or second flush; using very tender buds and shoots from an early season crop or more robust from later crops. Initially they are allowed to wither in a dark place, which reduces the water content. In China, the leaves are usually then roasted and left to dry out. This process kills the enzymes in the leaves, which prevents any oxidization. In Japan, this is more commonly achieved by steaming the leaves before they are rolled and dried.

80 per cent of the world's green tea comes from China, and as such the leaves have really interesting names. Two of my favourite green teas are Pi Lo Chun (which translates as 'jade snail spring') and Chun Mee (which translates as 'precious eyebrows'), both so named because of the shape of their leaves. The famous gunpowder tea traditionally used in Moroccan mint tea is also a green tea.

Japanese green teas such as gyokuro and sencha are gaining in popularity around the world, and matcha green tea powder, the tea traditionally used in Japanese tea ceremonies, is now widely used to flavour ice creams, noodles and cakes.

Research has uncovered amazing health benefits related to drinking green tea. Green teas are considered to have anti-aging and anti-bacterial properties. Drinking green tea on a regular basis can help to reduce levels of bad cholesterol in the body. As a natural source of antioxidants green tea is thought to help fight cancer, and investigations have also revealed that frequent consumption of green tea can aid weight loss.

A huge variety of flavoured green teas are now available to buy. I prefer to add my own natural flavourings to the tea – although I do love Jasmine tea, which is produced from an infusion of Jasmine flowers and green tea.

Oolong Tea

Oolong teas are partially oxidized, and therefore more processed than green tea but less so than black tea. They are essentially a hybrid of green and black tea, said to have been discovered by accident when a Chinese gardener was distracted by a deer that he subsequently killed and prepared to eat, forgetting about the tea that he had been brewing prior to his sudden diversion. Returning to the tea the next day, he found the leaves had changed colour due to partial oxidation – but he carried on and finished the tea anyway. The tea's increased aroma and depth of flavour made it a favourite – and so, oolong was born.

Oolong tea falls into two different categories. For darker oolongs, the leaves are tossed in bamboo drums to start the oxidization process. When they are 60–70 per cent oxidized, the leaves are dried. The lighter, greener oolongs are only 30 per cent oxidized and are wrapped in cloths and machine-rolled before being dried. Both have unique characteristics, and many tea aficionados believe oolongs to be the most distinctive and agreeable of all teas.

They are ideal for multiple steepings and it is said that the flavour of the tea gets better and better each time the pot is filled up. Dedicated oolong fans believe that the fourth or fifth steeping releases the best flavour – although you'd need a pretty strong bladder to get to your fifth cup without retiring.

Formosa oolong comes from Taiwan. Imperial formosa oolong is an especially acclaimed tea. Traditionally drunk by Taiwanese Buddhist monks, it is considered one of the best teas in the world.

Pu-erh Tea

Pu-erh teas are oxidized to a similar level as green teas, but are dark in colour and unique in that they go through a process known as post-fermentation. Traditionally, pu-erh comes from the Yunnan province in China and is gaining in popularity because one of its purported health benefits is that it is believed to aid weight loss. For 'raw' pu-erh, the processed tea is compressed into cakes and left to age for up to 50 years, making it very expensive. However, 'cooked' pu-erh is increasingly produced, which takes much less time to manufacture and involves the introduction of a special bacterial culture that speeds up the maturation.

Specialist tea suppliers will sell pu-erh tea cakes and bricks. The tea must be gently prised from the cake or brick, or the leaves will be damaged and this could have a negative effect on the flavour of the tea. The best tool to use for this delicate operation is a pu-erh knife, which is a special 'tea needle' that can be lightly inserted into the brick or cake and used to work the tea loose. However, loose leaf pu-erh is widely available from tea specialists, supermarkets , department stores and even health food shops.

White Tea

White tea is the least processed of all the teas and is generally the most esteemed. Only the topmost bud and leaves are picked from the bush, sometimes only the bud, and they are always first flush. The buds must be picked before they unfurl, are handled as little as possible and processed minimally. They are withered in the sunshine or, in bad weather, in a warm room. White teas are silvery in colour, have a mild flavour, are low in caffeine and have the highest antioxidant content of any of the teas.

Baihao yinzhen ('silver needle') and Pai Mutan, or Bai Mudan ('white peony') are particularly good white teas to look out for. Slightly sweet and deliciously mellow, silver needle is my own personal favourite tea.

YELLOW TEA

Yellow tea is produced in a similar way to green tea, but the leaves are left to turn yellow before they are dried. Yellow tea is generally milder and sweeter than green tea.

It is one of the rarest types of tea and is relatively undiscovered in the west. Yellow tea has a sweet, mellow flavour and is particular to the Sichuan and Hunan provinces of China. It may take a little effort to get hold of some, but as you begin to discover and enjoy the world of specialist teas, you will realize it's one worth tracking down!

TEA EQUIPMENT

Strictly speaking, the only essential things needed to make tea are a receptacle of some sort (a cup, mug or heatproof glass), some form of tea and boiled water (good-quality tea leaves tend to sink, so you shouldn't be struggling with too many stray leaves). Of course, if you're using a teabag, you'll need something to fish the tea bag out once your tea is brewed to the desired strength. But when you discover the world of truly amazing teas that are available, making the tea itself becomes a really enjoyable part of the whole process.

Pouring the tea from a beautiful pot is a delight, and filling up a favourite tea stick or tea ball or making your own-blend tea bag is a real pleasure, so there are various pieces of equipment you might like to invest in. Tea paraphernalia often also makes a great gift. Here are a few ideas you might like to consider.

TEAPOT

Once upon a time, a teapot was as much a piece of essential kitchen kit as the saucepan or pot. When the tea bag came along, things changed. If you think of the importance and ceremonies associated with tea around the world, it seems a shame that tea-making in the west was ever reduced to simply sticking a tea bag willy-nilly into a mug, pouring boiling water over it and squashing it with a spoon. Thankfully, proper tea is making a well deserved return to the table! Teapots come in all shapes and sizes and a variety of materials, from the very beautiful to the practical. I think they become a little like a favourite mug or cup and tea will definitely taste different depending on what pot it is made in. It would be a shame to serve a delicate white tea from the sort of traditional Brown Betty teapot that is customarily associated with a strong breakfast brew, but there is something about those sturdy teapots that make them perfect for on the table alongside a cooked breakfast and lots of hot buttery toast and marmalade.

I like to serve delicate white teas and green teas in pretty china pots that reflect their delicate flavour, although I love glass for the flowering tea balls. Glass teapots now have better insulation, so they keep the tea hot, and it's interesting to watch

Tea balls, Tea sticks and Infusers

Tea balls, tea sticks and infusers make it easy to brew loose-leaf tea while keeping the leaves contained, making them as convenient as tea bags while still allowing you to enjoy your favourite loose-leaf tea. However, some tea experts argue that they restrict the movement of the leaves and therefore don't allow the true characteristics of the tea to come out in the brewing process. They can be used in a teapot or individual mug or cup, and come in all shapes and sizes, from the plain and practical to the ornate. They are usually made from stainless steel, although they do come in silver, for those for whom cost isn't a consideration!

Tea Cosies

Just as the teapot was once a household item, so too was the tea cosy. Whether knitted, crocheted, sewn or shop bought, from the plain and practical to the entertaining and elaborate, the purpose of the tea cosy was to keep the pot warm. Sceptics argue that a tea cosy won't make much difference to keeping a pot hot, and, of course, tea left to sit could become over-brewed and bitter as the tannins continue to be released, but there is something fun and cheery about a tea cosy, so it's down to personal choice as to whether you have one (or several) in your personal *batterie de thé*!

Tea Caddies

Tea caddies, or canisters, have been around for as long as tea itself, and range from the everyday to the highly decorative, but essentially they do the necessary job of keeping the tea fresh, and therefore preserving its flavour. Premium teas

tea leaves or a tea ball unfurl as the brewing process takes place.

My everyday teapot is a sturdier earthenware pot that's a sort of white version of the Brown Betty. Of course, in an ideal world you would have a teapot to match the type of tea you are making. There are some beautiful Asian-style teapots with handles that somehow make drinking Japanese teas a very special experience, but not all of us have the budget or the cupboard space!

A good all-purpose pot would be made from not-too-delicate china. Some people favour the teapots that come with built-in infusers, so that the tea doesn't over-brew, but if you're worried about that, you can scoop the tea into an infuser and clip it to the side of the pot, then remove it when you're happy with the strength of the tea. Whatever the preference, there's a teapot out there for everyone.

can be bought in nice caddies, but are also increasingly sold in foil packages and ideally should be transferred to an airtight container upon opening.

STRAINERS, SQUEEZERS AND SUNDRIES

Pouring tea through a strainer into a cup does away with the risk of getting leaves in the cup and the embarrassment of trying to pick tea leaves out of your teeth. Good-quality tea leaves do sink to the bottom of the pot however, and so controlled pouring will help if you don't have a strainer to hand. They are inexpensive and easy to buy so a strainer is a good investment. Tea bag squeezers are a little bit of an indulgence, but they are a little more sophisticated than squashing the bag against the side of your cup with a spoon. There are also tea bag tidies, measuring and caddie spoons and all kinds of bits and bobs you can add to your kit as your enjoyment of fine teas unfolds.

HELPFUL TEA TERMINOLOGY

The science surrounding the harvesting, production, brewing and serving tea necessarily lends itself to a few pieces of jargon that you may come across when exploring the world of tea. As with wine and food, tea is often described by the accents of flavour found in the taste but there are also some technical terms that feature. Here are a few to get you started.

FANNINGS OR DUST

'Fannings' or 'dust' are mainly low-quality leftover leaves that are often used in tea bags.

FLOWERY

'Flowery' indicates that the tea includes buds and leaves, and is also a sign of good quality.

FLUSH

The term 'flush' is used to describe the tree's growing season, when it is pushing out new leaves. So a 'first flush' tea is produced using the very first tender buds and shoots, and is considered the most delicate in taste, although second flush tea leaves are thought to have a little more body. Subsequent flushes are used but generally not acknowledged.

ORANGE

Orange pekoe teas come under the orthodox black tea category and have a recognized grading system. Leaves are classified into larger leaf grades and 'broken' leaf grades, which are the smaller pieces. Legend has it that the term 'orange' came about when the East India Trading Company presented the tea to the Dutch royal family, the House of Orange, and subsequently went on to promote the tea as 'orange pekoe' to imply a royal warrant.

PICKING

'Picking', also known as 'plucking', happens between spring and autumn/fall, which is the growing season in countries such as China and northern India. In countries where the weather is more consistent, picking takes place all year round. The quality of the tea is determined by the number of leaves and buds that are plucked from each plant.

Tea can be graded by its country of origin – such as Darjeeling, Assam, China, Ceylon (Sri Lanka), and so on – but the grading of the leaves is also an important aspect of the tea-making process, as small leaves will brew at different rates to larger leaves and produce often very different results.

STEEPING

The essential process of soaking your tea leaves and ingredients in water. How you brew your tea comes down to personal preference but some teas, such as oolong are better suited to multiple steepings than others, and often result in an enhanced, richer flavour.

TIPPY

'Tippy' is an indication that the tea includes the highest proportion of buds, or 'tips', and is therefore of the highest quality.

BRINGING TEA TO THE TABLE

TEA PRODUCING REGIONS

From its origins in China all those centuries ago, major tea cultivation has now spread to the verdant hills, high mountains and coastal regions of a handful of countries. India, Japan, Sri Lanka and Taiwan join China as producers of the world's acclaimed teas.

CHINA

The humid tropical and subtropical provinces of southern China holds the largest concentration of the country's tea estates. China produces so much tea that the well-known phrase 'not for all the tea in China' came about - meaning 'not at any price', although India has now become the world's biggest producer of tea

INDIA

Assam and Darjeeling are often thought of types of tea, when in fact they are the regions in which those teas are cultivated. Darjeeling tea carries a PGi certificate, which means that only teas cultivated, produced and processed within a specified area of Darjeeling can actually carry the name. Genuine Darjeeling tea should carry the official logo, introduced by the Tea Board of India. Darjeeling teas were primarily black teas, but now green, oolong and white teas are increasingly being produced.

JAPAN

Tea was originally introduced to Japan from China by Buddhist monks. Nowadays, Japan is renowned for its excellent green teas and the Shizuoka and Kagoshima regions are the principal producers.

SRI LANKA

Formerly known as Ceylon, Sri Lanka's humidity, temperatures and rainfall all help to produce high quality teas. Sri Lankan teas are largely black, and the Sri Lankan Board of Tea issue a quality mark to pure Ceylon teas.

TAIWAN

Taiwan is an island situated off the south eastern coast of mainland China, originally known as Formosa. Because the bushes are cultivated at comparatively low altitudes, the island produced a high percentage of oolongs.

BREWING THE PERFECT CUPPA

Tea aficionados all around the world argue about how to brew the perfect cuppa, but loose tea is generally considered to produce a better quality tea than bags. Loose teas are most often produced from the whole leaf and allow the user more control over the strength of the tea; more leaves in the pot will usually make a stronger tea. Loose-leaf tea can usually be steeped several times; some teas are even thought to benefit from it. Real tea connoisseurs will pour an initial amount of hot water into a teapot containing the leaves, then pour the water out, rather than simply warming the pot before adding the leaves. The benefit of doing so is that any dust that is clinging to the leaves will be washed away, and the leaves are supposedly primed to swell, encouraging maximum flavour.

The Royal Society of Chemistry has published a guide to making the perfect cup of tea. They advise using freshly drawn water every time. When water boils, it loses some of its oxygen, and oxygen helps bring out the flavour of the tea. They recommend a ceramic teapot, as metal can sometimes taint the flavour of the tea.

The advice is to brew the tea for 3–4 minutes (although this would depend on the type of tea), since polyphenolic compounds (tannins) are released after this time which give the tea its colour and some of its flavour. However, leaving the tea to infuse for longer than this apparently introduces high molecular-weight tannins, which give the tea a bad aftertaste. I think this describes the bitter, over-brewed tea that we used to call 'stewed' in Yorkshire.

A Matter of Milk

Although many of the teas in this book are better without milk, the subject of when to add milk to teas that can take milk is a hotly contested one. Does the milk come first? Or the tea? Well, The Royal Society of Chemistry advocates that the milk (always fresh and chilled, and never long-lasting UHT) goes into the cup first, because degradation of the milk occurs if milk encounters temperatures above 75°C (167°F). The report says that 'if milk is poured into hot tea, individual drops separate from the bulk of the milk and come into contact with the high temperatures of the tea for enough time for significant denaturation to occur. This is much less likely to happen if hot water is added to the milk. Once full mixing has occurred, the temperature should be below 75°C (167°F).

Apparently, the perfect temperature at which to drink tea is 60–65°C (140–149°F) 'to avoid vulgar slurping which results from drinking tea at too high a temperature.'

The author of the report also goes on to say that 'to gain optimum ambience for enjoyment of tea, aim to achieve a seated drinking position, where quietness and calm will elevate the moment to a special dimension. For best results, carry a heavy bag of shopping – or walk the dog – in cold, driving rain for at least half an hour beforehand. This will make the tea taste out of this world.'

I hope that after reading this book and trying some of the teas, you will realize that tea can taste truly wonderful without having to haul heavy bags or schlep around the stormy streets beforehand!

BREAKFAST TEAS

Work-day breakfasts may well mean grabbing a quick bowl of cornflakes and speed-swishing a teabag around in a mug before slurping it down and heading out of the door, but when it comes to high days and holidays, it makes such a lovely change to slow down and take time to make something special to share with family or friends. Start the day with homemade chia seed muffins, fresh from the pan crumpets, or even a slice of gorgeous just-baked tart. And instead of that ever-so-slightly humdrum cuppa, why not try one of a world of delicious teas. And to think the day has only just begun!

orange pekoe tea with fat rascals

Despite the name, orange pekoe doesn't actually contain any orange.
Orange pekoe is a term largely used to describe a category of black teas
noted for their high quality, which mostly come from India and Sri Lanka.
I first ate fat rascals in Harrogate, North Yorkshire, at Betty's Café Tea
Rooms, but at the time they wouldn't divulge the recipe, so I bought one and
did a bit of an autopsy on it at home. Here's what I came up with.

150 g/1 cup plus
   2 tablespoons plain/
   all-purpose flour
150 g/1 cup plus
   2 tablespoons self-
   raising/rising flour
1 teaspoon baking powder
130 g/9 tablespoons butter,
   cubed
90 g/scant ½ cup caster/
   superfine sugar
grated zest of 1 orange
grated zest of 1 lemon
1 teaspoon ground
   cinnamon
½ teaspoon freshly grated
   nutmeg
150 g/1 generous cup
   mixed dried fruit
   (I use currants, raisins
   and sultanas)
1 egg, beaten
50 ml/3 tablespoons milk
1 egg yolk
a pinch of salt
glacé cherries and
   blanched almonds,
   to decorate

Makes 6

Preheat the oven to 200°C (400°F) Gas 6.

Sift both flours and the baking powder into a large bowl. Add the butter and rub into the flour until the mixture resembles fine breadcrumbs.

Add the sugar, orange and lemon zests, spices and dried fruit and mix well. Add the beaten egg and enough milk to bring the mixture together to a soft dough. Shape the mixture into 6 saucer-sized rounds, about 2 cm (5 in) deep.

Mix the egg yolk, 1 tablespoon water and salt together to make a glaze and brush this over the fat rascals. Decorate with the cherries and almonds. Transfer to a non-stick baking sheet and bake for 15–20 minutes, or until golden brown.

Fat rascals are best served warm, either alone or with plenty of butter. They're also gorgeous served with vanilla-scented mascarpone.

For 1 pot of tea
3–4 teaspoons orange pekoe tea
sugar or honey, to taste
milk, to taste

Warm the pot and add the tea leaves. Pour in boiling water and leave to brew for about 4 minutes. Sweeten with sugar or honey and add milk, if desired.

Moroccan Mint Tea
with Apple, Cinnamon and Cardamom Bourekas

Traditionally, Moroccan mint tea is brewed in a very specific way: the leaves are washed and the water is poured into the pot from a certain height, as is the tea, once brewed. This process adds oxygen, which is believed to draw out more flavour. Bourekas are crisp, golden little pastry parcels. Here I've used apple, cinnamon and cardamom: perfect for breakfast with the mint tea.

400 g/14 oz. crisp
   dessert apples
60 g/5 tablespoons butter
5 cardamom pods
50 g/¼ cup caster/
   superfine sugar
a pinch of salt
1 teaspoon ground
   cinnamon
grated zest and juice
   of 1 small lemon
8 sheets of filo/phyllo
   pastry squares, about
   20 x 20 cm/8 x 8 in
1 teaspoon caster/
   superfine sugar
2 tablespoons chia seeds

Makes 8

Preheat the oven to 190°C (375°F) Gas 5.

Peel and core the apples and cut them into smallish dice. Melt half the butter in a large frying pan or wok and add the diced apples. Remove the seeds from the cardamom pods. Stir in the sugar, salt, cardamom seeds and cinnamon. Cook for about 5 minutes, or until the apples have turned golden and the juices have started to thicken. Add the lemon zest and juice and cook for 3–4 minutes, until the apples are soft. Remove from the heat and allow to cool.

In the meantime, take a sheet of filo/phyllo pastry and fold it in half, so that you have a rectangle two layers thick. Melt the remaining butter in a small saucepan. Brush the pastry lightly with butter. Place a tablespoon of the cooked, cooled apple in the bottom left-hand corner of the pastry. Lift the corner beneath it and pull it over the filling to form a triangle. Fold the pastry immediately to the left, so that it retains the triangle shape. Repeat the process, folding up and down, until the pastry is used up and you are left with a neat triangle. Place it on a non-stick baking sheet and brush lightly with butter. Repeat to make 7 more bourekas. Sprinkle each one with sugar and chia seeds and bake in the oven for about 8–10 minutes, until crisp and golden.

For 1 Pot of Tea
2 teaspoons green tea
a handful of fresh mint

Warm a teapot. Add the tea and mint and fill with boiling water. Allow to brew for about 3 minutes. Remove the mint and pour into cups.

Assam Leaf Tea
with Goji Berry, Chia Seed and Marmalade Muffins

Assam tea is one of the oldest varieties in the world; the bushes originally grew wild on the immense flood plains of the Brahmaputra River in the Assam region of India. Today, the steamy, hot conditions of the region still produce rich, full-bodied tea with distinctive small leaves and a malty flavour that makes it popular at breakfast time. Chewy red goji berries and crunchy chia seeds are full of antioxidants and other good stuff, and the bonus is that they taste really great. I love them sprinkled over a bowl of fruit and yoghurt for weekday breakfasts, but for a weekend treat, I make these lovely muffins and serve them with a seasonal fruit compote. On less virtuous days I just eat them warm from the oven with a generous slathering of butter. And a pot of good tea is never far away!

160 g/1¼ cups plain/
all-purpose flour
2 teaspoons baking powder
50 g/¼ cup caster/
superfine sugar
30 g/¼ cup chia seeds
50 g/⅓ cup dried goji
berries
1 egg
100 ml/6½ tablespoons
milk
1 teaspoon pure vanilla
extract
100 g/6½ tablespoons
butter, melted and
cooled slightly
50 g/3 tablespoons fine-
cut orange marmalade

*a 6-cup muffin pan,
or 6 freestanding muffin
papers, lightly greased*

Makes 6

Preheat the oven to 180°C (350°F) Gas 4. Put the flour, baking powder and sugar in a large bowl and mix well. Add the chia seeds and goji berries and stir them in.

In a separate bowl, beat the egg, milk and vanilla extract together. Add the slightly cooled butter and beat again.

Gently but carefully mix the egg mixture into the dry ingredients, until fully incorporated. Spoon the mixture into the prepared moulds.

Bake for about 20 minutes, until the muffins are risen and golden and spring back when pressed lightly.

In the meantime, warm the marmalade a little in a small saucepan. Remove the muffins from the oven and leave to cool slightly before brushing the tops with a light glaze of marmalade.

Serve warm with a pot of Assam tea.

For 1 Pot of Tea
*3-4 teaspoons Assam tea leaves
sugar or honey, to taste*

Warm the pot and add the tea leaves. Pour in the boiling water, stir and leave to brew for 3–4 minutes. Sweeten with sugar or honey and serve with the warm muffins.

JASMINE GREEN TEA PEARLS WITH PAN DE SAL

There's something magical about the combination of warm pan de sal, a traditional, light-as-air sweet bread with distinctive breadcrumb topping from the Philippines, and fragrant jasmine tea. To make the tea pearls, tippy green tea leaves are layered with jasmine blossoms and hand-rolled into tiny spheres.

150 ml/⅔ cup evaporated milk

125 g/1 stick butter

150 ml/⅔ cup whole milk

23 g/¾ oz. fresh yeast

120 g/⅔ cup caster/ superfine sugar

1 egg, beaten

600 g/4⅔ cups plain/ all-purpose flour, plus extra for dusting

¾ teaspoon salt

50 g/⅔ cup fine dried breadcrumbs

butter, to serve

2 heavy baking sheets, greased

MAKES 12

Pour 150 ml (⅔ cup) water and the evaporated milk into a saucepan or pot and add the butter. Heat gently until the butter has melted. Remove and cool slightly, then pour in the whole milk.

Cream together the yeast and 1 teaspoon of the sugar in a small bowl. Once smooth, pour in a little of the cooled milk mixture and stir until well mixed. Stir in the beaten egg.

Put the flour, remaining sugar and salt in a large bowl and mix well. Gradually pour the milk mixture into the flour while stirring. Continue until you have a smooth, sticky dough. Turn it out onto a clean work surface lightly dusted with flour. Knead for 6–7 minutes, until the dough loses its stickiness. Add a little extra flour if needed, but don't go too mad or the bread will become heavy. Put into a bowl, cover and leave in a warm place for about 45 minutes.

Turn the dough out onto a clean, floured work surface and knead for 3–4 minutes, until smooth. Flatten it out to make a 10 x 30 cm (4 x 2 in) rectangle, then roll to make a log shape. Put the breadcrumbs in a shallow tray. Cut the dough into 12 slices about 1 cm (½ in) thick. Gently coat each slice in the breadcrumbs and place on the prepared baking sheets, well spaced out. Leave to prove/rise until doubled in size, for another 45 minutes–1 hour. About 20 minutes before the end of the second rising time, preheat the oven to 200°C (400°F) Gas 6. Bake the pan de sal for about 10-15 minutes, until golden brown and firm.

FOR 1 POT OF TEA

1 teaspoon Jasmine green tea pearls
honey or sugar, to taste

Warm the teapot and add the jasmine pearls. Pour over boiled and slightly cooled water, then infuse for 5–6 minutes. Sweeten with honey as desired. This is definitely a tea to drink without milk.

500 g/4 cups self-raising/rising
flour, plus extra for dusting

100 g/6½ tablespoons butter,
diced

a pinch of salt

50 g/¼ cup caster/ superfine sugar

½ teaspoon ground cinnamon

1 Bramley apple, peeled, cored
and diced

scant 300 ml/1¼ cups whole milk

1 egg and 1 tablespoon milk,
beaten together

a 4-cm/1½-in cookie cutter

Makes 6-8

PRINCE OF WALES TEA
WITH APPLE AND CINNAMON SCONES

Prince of Wales tea is a blend of black China tea originally created for Edward, Prince of Wales (the future King Edward VIII). In 1921, he granted Twinings permission to sell his personal blend using his royal title and they have done so ever since. It's quite a mild tea with a strong aroma, and it makes a perfect cuppa. These lovely apple scones make a very regal combination with the tea.

Preheat the oven to 200°C (400°F) Gas 6.

Sieve the flour into a large bowl and add the butter. Rub it lightly into the flour with your fingertips, lifting the mixture to aerate it as you work. When the mixture resembles fine breadcrumbs, add the salt, sugar and cinnamon and mix to combine. Stir in the apple.

Add just enough milk to bring the mixture together to form a soft (but not sticky) dough. Take care not to handle the dough too much or the scones will become heavy.

Lightly dust a clean work surface with flour and roll the dough out to about 3 cm (1 in) thick. Stamp out rounds with the cookie cutter. Try to avoid re-rolling the dough, as this will make the scones heavy. Place the scones on a non-stick baking sheet and bake for about 12–15 minutes, until risen and golden. Leave to cool a little on a wire rack. They are lovely served warm.

FOR 1 POT OF TEA

3 Prince of Wales tea bags
sugar or honey, to taste
milk, to taste

Warm the pot. Add the tea bags and pour boiling water over. Leave to brew for 2–5 minutes. Sweeten and add milk as desired.

Passion Fruit and Orange Tea
with Sticky Oat Breakfast Bars

*If you like fruity notes in your tea now and again there are some really nice blends on the market.
I'm not a big fan of the shop-bought fruity infusions that don't include tea as a base, but Lipton make
a very nice green tea that is delicately flavoured with passion fruit, jasmine and orange, and other
companies make a similar blend. These sticky oat bars are easy to make and packed with oats and seeds,
so they make a great accompaniment to a cuppa for those of us who aren't big on breakfast, or are a little
short on time in the mornings.*

225 g/scant 1 cup butter

225 g/1 cup plus 2
tablespoons brown sugar

3 tablespoons honey

a pinch of salt

325 g/3¼ cups jumbo oats

2 tablespoons mixed seeds
(such as sunflower,
sesame, hemp, pumpkin
or linseeds)

50 g/1 cup cornflakes

*a 20 x 30-cm/8 x 12-in
baking pan, greased and
lined with baking
parchment*

Makes 15

Preheat the oven to 180°C (350°F) Gas 4.

Melt the butter, sugar, honey and salt together in a saucepan over
gentle heat. Stir in the oats, seeds and cornflakes.

Spoon the mixture into the prepared pan and bake for 20–25 minutes,
until golden and firm.

Leave to cool in the pan, then cut into squares.

For 1 Pot of Tea

*1 passion fruit and orange tea bag per person
sugar or honey, to taste*

Put a tea bag in each mug and pour over boiling water.
Leave to brew for 2–5 minutes. Sweeten with sugar
or honey, as desired.

Yunnan Tea
with Brioche Pancakes and Apricot Compote

A black tea from Yunnan province in China, this tea has a naturally sweet flavour with slightly nutty overtones. You can drink Yunnan tea with or without milk, although I suggest brewing for less time if drinking without milk, to give it a lighter flavour. These deliciously different pancakes make a fantastic weekend brunch, and a pot of Yunnan tea to accompany them makes a special start to the day.

For the Pancakes
3 eggs, separated
300 ml/1¼ cups soured cream
75 g/⅓ cup caster/superfine sugar
40 g/3 tablespoons butter, melted, plus extra for frying
1 teaspoon vanilla extract
200 ml/¾ cup milk
200 g/6½ oz. brioche
2 tablespoons self-raising/rising flour
75 g/⅔ cup sultanas/golden raisins

For the Compote
150 g/¾ cup caster/granulated sugar
450 g/16 oz. fresh apricots, halved and stoned/pitted
25 g/2 tablespoons butter
icing/confectioners' sugar, to dust

Serves 4

Put the egg yolks in a large bowl with the soured cream, sugar, melted butter, vanilla extract and milk. Beat until smooth. Cut the brioche into small cubes and add to the mix. Leave to stand for about 15 minutes, to allow the brioche to soak up some of the batter. Using a slotted spoon, remove the soaked pieces of brioche to a separate bowl and set aside. Add the flour to the batter mix and stir well. Return the brioche to the bowl, add the sultanas/golden raisins and mix well. Whisk the egg whites until stiff, and then fold this gently into the mixture.

Heat a heavy-based frying pan and brush it lightly with melted butter. Place tablespoons of the mixture into the pan, leaving some space between them. Cook the pancakes for 2–3 minutes, until bubbles appear on the surface of each one. Carefully flip the pancakes over and cook for a further 2–3 minutes, until golden brown.

For the compote, put 5 tablespoons water and the sugar in a saucepan and bring to the boil, stirring to dissolve the sugar. Add the apricots to the pan and turn the heat down. Simmer for 3–4 minutes, until the apricots have softened. Leave to cool.

Serve the pancakes dusted with icing/confectioners' sugar, with the apricot compote alongside.

For 1 Pot of Tea
3–4 teaspoons Yunnan tea leaves
sugar or honey, to taste
milk, to taste

Warm the pot and add the tea leaves. Pour in the boiling water, stir and leave to brew for 3–4 minutes. Add milk as desired and sweeten with sugar or honey.

BUILDERS' TEA
WITH CRUMPETS

There's a legend that suggests all builders ever want to drink is strong tea with milk and about four sugars. But we all have our favourite brand of this sort of tea – generally black tea, often made from lower-grade leaves and fannings, or dustings – and sometimes it's just what we fancy. Builders' tea has a gutsy flavour and makes a good cuppa to start the day, especially alongside warm, freshly made crumpets with lashings of good butter.

350 ml/1½ cups milk
250 g/2 cups plain/
   all-purpose flour
a pinch of salt
2 teaspoons caster/granulated sugar
7 g/2 teaspoons dried fast-
   action/active yeast

½ teaspoon baking powder
1 tablespoon melted butter, plus
   extra for frying

metal crumpet rings

MAKES 8

Heat the milk in a saucepan until it is lukewarm. Mix the flour, salt and sugar together in a large bowl. Add the yeast and baking powder. Stir the butter and milk together, then pour it into the flour. Stir well and leave to rise for about 1 hour.

Grease the base of a frying pan with butter, set it over medium heat and pop the crumpet rings into it. Spoon a little batter into each one and cook for a couple of minutes, until the mixture starts to set, little bubbles appear at the top and the bases are golden. Carefully remove the rings and turn the crumpets over. Cook for a further 2–3 minutes, until firm and golden. Wrap them in a clean dish cloth to keep them warm, and make the others in the same way. Serve warm with lots of butter and jam/jelly. To reheat, simply pop them in a toaster or cook under a hot grill/broiler.

FOR 1 POT OF TEA
2–3 tea bags
milk and sugar, to taste

Warm the teapot and add the tea bags. Pour over boiling water and leave to brew for 3–4 minutes. Add milk and sugar to taste.

Rooibos Red Tea
with Candied Fruit Blintzes and Blackcurrant Sauce

Rooibos means 'red bush' in Afrikaans. It's not a tea, but a plant grown in the Western Cape of South Africa. The leaves produce a red tea with a slightly sweet and nutty flavour. High in antioxidants and naturally caffeine-free, it's very good for you, especially so alongside these glorious little pancake packages!

For the blintzes
2 eggs

300 ml/1¼ cups milk

40 g/3 tablespoons butter, melted, plus extra for brushing

40 g/3 tablespoons sugar

a pinch of salt

130 g/generous 1 cup plain/all-purpose flour

35 g/2½ tablespoons butter

For the filling
350 g/12 oz. cream cheese

50 g/¼ cup caster/granulated sugar

2 egg yolks

1 tablespoon orange liqueur

grated zest of 1 orange

120 g/1 cup finely diced good-quality candied fruit

For the sauce
175 g/¾ cup good-quality blackcurrant jam/jelly

50 g/3 tablespoons butter, melted

an ovenproof dish, greased

Serves 4

First of all, make the blintzes. Place the eggs, milk and melted butter into a food processor or blender. Add the sugar and salt and whizz until everything is well mixed. Add the flour and whizz again until you have a smooth batter. Set aside for 30 minutes, if possible.

Butter a non-stick frying pan or crêpe pan and set it over medium-high heat until very hot. Pour in a small amount of batter and tilt the pan to spread the mixture evenly over the base. Cook for 1–2 minutes, until the blintz is golden underneath and set and bubbly on top. Gently loosen it with a palette knife and turn it over. Cook for another minute, until golden brown. Repeat to make 8 blintzes.

To make the filling, beat the cream cheese, sugar, egg yolks, liqueur and orange zest together in a large bowl. Add the candied fruit.

Preheat the oven to 180°C (350°F) Gas 4. Lay a blintz out flat and put a generous spoonful of filling in the centre. Fold in the sides, then fold in the top and the bottom to form a parcel. Turn it over and place in the ovenproof dish, seam side down. Repeat with the remaining blintzes. Brush generously with melted butter. Cover the dish with kitchen foil and bake for 15 minutes or so, until heated through.

In the meantime, make the sauce. Put the jam/jelly and 3 tablespoons water in a small saucepan and heat gently, stirring constantly.

Serve the blintzes, hot from the oven with the sauce poured over them.

For 1 pot of tea
3 teaspoons rooibos tea (or tea bags)
sugar or honey, to taste

Warm the teapot and add the tea. Pour over boiling water. Stir gently and leave to infuse for 3–4 minutes. Sweeten to taste. In South Africa, rooibos is often served with lemon and sugar (or honey), but without milk.

ROYAL ENGLISH BREAKFAST TEA
WITH TRADITIONAL FRUIT TEA BREAD

English breakfast tea is usually a blend of black teas such as Assam, Ceylon and Kenya, although some tea companies prefer to use only Assam. Breakfast tea is usually quite strong and gutsy with malty, nutty overtones. It's one of the few teas I believe actually benefits from the addition of milk. Of course, English breakfast tea makes a great accompaniment to the classic English breakfast, but it's also really good with this lovely fruit tea bread, which I love to serve toasted and slathered with lots of butter.

350 g/3 cups mixed dried fruit

300 ml/1¼ cups freshly brewed Earl Grey tea, hot

400 g/3¼ cups self-raising/rising flour

1 teaspoon baking powder

1 egg, beaten

a 900-g/2-lb. loaf tin, lightly greased and lined with baking parchment

MAKES 10–12 SLICES

Put the fruit in a large bowl and pour over the hot tea. Cover and leave to stand for several hours, preferably overnight.

When you are ready to bake the loaf, preheat the oven to 180°C (350°F) Gas 4. Sieve the flour and baking powder together into a large bowl. Add the soaked fruit and stir well. Beat in the egg until everything is thoroughly combined.

Pour the mixture into the prepared tin and bake for about 1½ hours, or until a skewer inserted into the centre of the loaf comes out clean.

Leave to cool for 15 minutes or so, and then turn out onto a wire rack to cool completely.

FOR 1 POT OF TEA
3–4 teaspoons English Breakfast tea or tea bags
milk and sugar, to taste

Warm the pot. Add the tea bags and pour over boiling water. Leave to brew for 2-5 minutes. Sweeten to taste with sugar or honey and add milk as desired.

Mango-Infused Tippy Green Tea
With Fresh Apricot Tart

One of the leading factors in determining the flavour and caffeine content of a tea is the proportion of tips or leaf buds it contains. Tippy teas generally have a smoother, milder flavour and a higher caffeine content than teas with larger, mature leaves. Here, I've added dried mango to tippy green tea to give a subtle hint of fruitiness – an ideal match for a fresh apricot tart.

For the Pastry
175 g/1½ sticks soft butter
50 g/¼ cup caster/
 superfine sugar
a pinch of salt
1 egg yolk
250 g/2 cups plain/
 all-purpose flour

For the Filling
120 g/1 stick soft butter
a pinch of salt
120 g/⅔ cup caster/
 superfine sugar
2 eggs
120 g/1 cup ground
 almonds/almond meal
750 g/1 lb. 10 oz. fresh,
 ripe (but firm) apricots,
 quartered and
 stoned/pitted
5 tablespoons smooth
 apricot jam/jelly

a 23-cm/9-in tart pan with
 removable base, and
 baking beans

Serves 6–8

Preheat the oven to 180°C (350°F) Gas 4.

For the pastry, beat the butter, sugar and salt together until smooth. Add the egg yolk and stir until thoroughly mixed. Fold in the flour and bring it all together to form a smooth dough. Wrap in clingfilm/plastic wrap and set aside in a cool place while preparing the filling.

For the filling, beat the butter, salt and sugar together until light and fluffy. Stir in the eggs and beat until fully combined. Add the almonds and stir until they are fully incorporated and the mixture is smooth.

Roll out the pastry and use it to line the tart pan. Trim of the excess. Line the pan with the pastry and trim off the excess. Line with baking paper, fill with baking beans and bake the pastry blind for about 10 minutes, or until light golden and firm. Allow to cool.

Spread the filling in an even layer over the tart base. Arrange the apricots over the filling, facing up in concentric circles and close together. Bake the tart for about 45 minutes, until the filling is firm and golden. Remove from the oven and allow to cool. Finally, warm the apricot jam/ jelly with 1 tablespoon water and brush it all over the apricots for a shiny glaze.

For 1 Pot of Tea
4 teaspoons tippy green tea
2 tablespoons thinly sliced dried mango

Warm a teapot. Add the tea and mango and fill with boiling water. Allow to brew for 4–5 minutes. Pour into tea glasses and add an extra slice of mango if desired.

CALMING TEAS

These days, it's so easy to get caught up in the hustle and bustle
of everyday life. So often the day disappears and we haven't realised
just how much pressure we've put upon ourselves. It's so nice every
now and then, just to put the brakes on and relax. Of course
sometimes we need a little help to wind down – and here are some
great teas and tisanes which help do just that. Of course if you
happen to have an irresistible banana and nutmeg custard brownie,
or a crisp cardamom shortbread as an accompaniment… well then,
you'll be laid back and in heaven all at the same time!

CHAMOMILE FLOWER TEA
WITH VANILLA BUTTER COOKIES

Chamomile flowers are renowned for their calming and digestive properties. There are many brands of chamomile infusions, and you can create your own with dried chamomile flowers. These little buttery, vanilla-speckled cookies go well with any kind of chamomile tea.

2 vanilla pods
200 g/1¾ sticks soft butter
100 g/½ cup caster/
    superfine sugar, plus
    extra for dusting
300 g/2¼ cups plain/
    all-purpose flour

*2–3 cookie sheets, lined with
    baking parchment*

MAKES 20-25

Preheat the oven to 180°C (350°F) Gas 4.

Split the vanilla pods lengthwise and scrape out the seeds. Cream the butter, vanilla seeds and sugar until smooth, then stir in the flour until fully combined.

Break off pieces of dough about the size of a walnut and roll each one into a ball. Place on the prepared cookie sheets, leaving a little gap between each to allow for slight spreading. Push the tines of a fork into the dough to flatten it slightly and bake for about 10–13 minutes, until golden and firm. Dust with caster sugar.

Transfer to a wire rack to cool. Store in an airtight container until ready to serve.

FOR 1 POT OF TEA
*2 teaspoons dried chamomile flowers
honey or sugar, to taste*

Warm a teapot and add the chamomile. Fill with boiling water and infuse for 5 minutes. Sweeten as desired.

Rooibos and Vanilla Tea
with Banana and Nutmeg, Custard Brownies

The slightly sweet and nutty flavour of rooibos is complemented by vanilla; I think the two make a perfect combination. Pair a cup or two with these deliciously different brownies and the stresses of the world just fade away…You can buy rooibos teabags already infused with vanilla, but it's easy to make using fresh tea and a vanilla pod too, whichever you prefer.

20 g/4 teaspoons butter
450 g/2¼ cups caster/
　superfine sugar
50 g/1½ oz. dark chocolate
100 g/¾ cup cocoa powder
4 eggs, beaten
100 g/¾ cup plain/
　all-purpose flour
1 teaspoon baking powder
2 very ripe bananas,
　mashed

For the Custard Layer
250 g/1 cup mascarpone
4 egg yolks
100 g/½ cup caster/
　superfine sugar
freshly grated nutmeg

*a 20 x 30-cm/8 x 12-in
　rectangular roasting pan
　or cake pan, lightly
　greased*

Makes 15

Preheat the oven to 180°C (350°F) Gas 4.

Melt the butter, sugar, chocolate and cocoa powder together in a large heatproof bowl set over a pan of barely simmering water, or heat gently in a microwave. Remove from the heat and leave to cool slightly.

Stir in the eggs. Add the flour and baking powder and stir again until smooth. Add the mashed banana and mix well. Pour the mixture into the prepared pan.

For the custard layer, beat the mascarpone, egg yolks and sugar together until smooth. Drizzle the mixture randomly across the chocolate layer. Scatter the custard mixture with grated nutmeg. Bake for about 35 minutes, until firm but still slightly fudgy.

Leave to cool in the pan, then cut into squares.

For 1 pot of tea
*3 teaspoons rooibos tea (or use tea bags)
1 plump vanilla pod
sugar or honey, to taste*

Warm the teapot and add the tea. Fill it with boiling water. Split the vanilla pod lengthwise and scrape out the seeds. Add them to the pot along with the pod. Give everything a gentle stir and leave to infuse for 3–4 minutes. Sweeten to taste and pour into cups.

FOR THE SHORTCRUST
150 g/1 cup plus
  2 tablespoons plain/
  all-purpose flour, plus
  extra for dusting
150 g/1 stick plus
  2 tablespoons butter
75 g/⅓ cup caster/
  superfine sugar
75 g/½ cup plus
  1 tablespoon rice flour
grated zest of ½ lemon

FOR THE FILLING
1 vanilla pod
2 egg yolks
200 g/scant 1 cup clotted
  cream
80 g/⅓ cup caster/
  superfine sugar
a pinch of flaky sea salt
250 g/2 cups fresh
  raspberries
3 tablespoons icing/
  confectioners' sugar

6 tartlet pans with
  removable base, about
  1 cm/2.5 in diameter
a cooks' blow torch

MAKES 6

LEMON BALM TEA
WITH CLOTTED CREAM AND RASPBERRY BRÛLÉE TARTLETS

Lemon balm has a lovely, delicate lemon flavour and is known for its calming properties. If you have some in the garden, making this delightful, gently aromatic tea will be easy: just infuse some green or white tea with a few of the leaves. I've paired it with these delicious little tarts; it's a combination I love to serve on sunny summer afternoons.

Preheat the oven to 180°C (350°F) Gas 4.

Rub together the flour, butter, sugar and rice flour until the mixture looks like breadcrumbs. Stir in the lemon zest and bring it together to form a dough. Chill until firm, then roll out on a lightly floured surface and line the pans, then return them to the fridge to chill.

Split the vanilla pods lengthwise and scrape out the seeds. Beat the egg yolks, clotted cream, sugar, vanilla seeds and salt until smooth.

Bake the shortcrust bases for 6–8 minutes, until firm and pale golden. If the shortcrust has risen up slightly, simply push it back carefully against the edges with a teaspoon. Remove from the oven and scatter the raspberries over the bases. Pour in the custard filling. Bake for 8–10 minutes for the fairy cake size, or 10–15 minutes for the larger size. Remove from the oven and leave to cool.

Sprinkle a fine layer of icing/confectioners' sugar over the top of each tart and caramelize carefully with a blow torch, taking care not to burn any raspberries that may be peeping out of the custard. Serve within a couple of hours, so that the brûlée top remains crisp.

FOR 1 POT OF TEA
3-4 teaspoons green or white tea, or tea bags
small handful lemon balm leaves
honey or sugar, to taste

Warm the pot and add the tea. Add the lemon balm leaves and pour over boiled, slightly cooled water. Infuse for 5 minutes. Sweeten as desired.

African Honeybush Tea
With Orange and Rosemary Cake

Honeybush is a cousin of rooibos, and therefore not technically a true tea. Just like rooibos, it is cultivated in South Africa's Eastern Cape and Western Cape provinces. Honeybush has a similar flavour, but is slightly sweeter, and is also caffeine free. Its name derives from the blossoms of the bush, which smell of honey. Sweetening the tea with honey adds a further depth of flavour, and eating a slice of this lovely orange and rosemary cake with it makes it even better!

320 g/2½ cups plain/
   all-purpose flour
2 teaspoons baking powder
150 g/¾ cup caster/
   superfine sugar
3 eggs
200 ml/¾ cup whole milk
120 g/1 stick butter,
   melted and cooled
grated zest of 2 oranges
   and juice of 1
1 tablespoon finely
   chopped fresh rosemary
4 tablespoons marmalade

*a 20-cm/8-in cake pan with
   removable base, greased
   and lined with baking
   parchment*

SERVES 8-10

Preheat the oven to 180°C (350°F) Gas 4.

Sieve the flour and baking powder into a large bowl. Stir in the sugar.

In a separate bowl, whisk the eggs and milk together with the cooled melted butter. Stir lightly but thoroughly into the flour mixture. Stir in the orange zest and juice, taking care not to overmix. Fold in the chopped rosemary needles.

Spoon the mixture into the prepared cake pan and bake for 50–55 minutes, until the cake has risen and is golden brown, and a skewer inserted into the centre comes out clean.

Leave to cool in the pan for 20 minutes or so, then turn out onto a wire rack and leave to cool completely.

Push the marmalade through a fine sieve/strainer and heat it gently in a small saucepan or pot. Brush the mixture evenly over the cake. Store in an airtight container.

> ### For 1 Pot of Tea
> *3–4 teaspoons African honeybush tea
> honey, to taste*
>
> Warm the pot and add the tea. Pour over boiling water and leave to brew for 5–6 minutes. Sweeten with honey.

Olive Leaf Tea
with Pine Nut and Rosemary Cookies

Olive leaf tea is an unusual, soothing sort of brew. It is said to have all kinds of amazing health benefits; the jury is still out on this one, but given the amazing health properties that olives contain, it seems reasonable to think that Mother Nature might have squeezed a few good things into the leaves as well. These crunchy pine nut cookies with just a hint of rosemary are delicious and so easy to make.

100 g/¾ cup pine nuts
120 g/1 stick soft butter
100 g/½ cup caster/
   superfine sugar
a pinch of salt
1 teaspoon very finely
   chopped fresh rosemary
150 g/1 cup plus 2
   tablespoons plain/all-
   purpose flour

Makes 15

Preheat the oven to 180°C (350°F) Gas 4.

Put the pine nuts in a large pan over medium heat and cook for 2–3 minutes, until toasted and golden, stirring regularly to prevent them burning. Remove and leave to cool.

Beat the butter, sugar and salt together until light and fluffy. Add the chopped rosemary and flour and stir until it is fully incorporated and the mixture is smooth. Add the pine nuts and stir to combine.

Place tablespoons of the mixture on a non-stick cookie sheet, spaced out well to allow room for the cookies to spread. Bake for about 8–10 minutes, until golden and firm. Remove from the heat and transfer to a wire rack to cool. The cookies will crisp up as they cool. Store in an airtight container until ready to serve.

For 1 Pot of Tea

1 heaped teaspoon olive leaf tea leaves
   (a little goes a long way)
sugar or honey, to taste

Warm the teapot and add the tea. Pour over boiling water and brew for 5 minutes. Serve with sugar or honey to sweeten.

Manuka Honey Tea
with Honey and Banana Bread

Manuka honey is a wonderful product with lots of health-giving properties, and makes a lovely sweetener for tea. Simply make a pot of green tea and sweeten with honey to taste, but let the water cool slightly first, as boiling water is said to destroy some of the benefits. For days when you want a quick cuppa, Clipper makes manuka honey tea bags, which are very nice. This cake is lovely served just as it is, but a layer of cold, creamy butter definitely lifts it to another level.

120 g/1 stick butter

100 g/½ cup caster/ superfine sugar

4 tablespoons runny honey

2 eggs, beaten

250 g/2 cups self-raising/ rising flour

2 very ripe bananas, mashed

a 900-g/2-lb. loaf pan, greased and lined with baking parchment

Serves 6

Preheat the oven to 180°C (350°F) Gas 4.

Put the butter and sugar in a large bowl and beat until smooth and light. Add the honey and beat well. Add the eggs, a little a time – you can add a little flour too, if the mixture curdles. Stir in the remaining flour, and then the mashed bananas.

Spoon the mixture into the prepared pan and bake for about 1 hour 15 minutes, until it has risen and is golden and a skewer inserted into the centre comes out clean.

Leave the cake to cool in the pan for 20 minutes or so, then turn out onto a wire rack and leave to cool completely.

For 1 Pot of Tea

*3–4 teaspoons green tea leaves
(or use 3 manuka honey tea bags)
manuka honey, to taste*

Warm the pot and add the tea. Pour over boiling water and leave to brew for 3–4 minutes. Sweeten to taste with manuka honey.

Kaffir Lime Leaf Tea
with Caramelized Pear and Thyme Cake

Kaffir lime leaves add a lovely flavour to tea; I often use them to add flavour to a pot of white tea. Fresh leaves are best for this recipe, and you should be able find them quite easily in Asian food stores. At a pinch you could use dried, which are often found in the Asian section of major supermarkets, but the flavour isn't quite as fresh and pronounced. This pear cake is sticky and lovely, and the fragrant tea makes a perfect match.

280 g/2 sticks plus
  3 tablespoons butter
280 g/1½ cups caster/
  superfine sugar, plus
  extra for dusting
4 firm but ripe pears,
  peeled, cored and diced
4 eggs, beaten
280 g/2¼ cups self-
  raising/rising flour
1 tablespoon fresh thyme
  leaves

*a 20 x 30-cm/9 x 5-in deep
  roasting pan or cake pan,
  lightly greased*

Makes 10

Preheat the oven to 180°C (350°F) Gas 4.

Place 30 g (1¼ oz.) of the butter and 30 g (1¼ oz.) of the sugar in a non-stick frying pan over medium heat and cook until the sugar has dissolved. Add the diced pear and cook for about 5–8 minutes, until the pear is golden and caramelized. Leave to cool a little.

Beat the remaining butter and sugar together until light and fluffy. Add the eggs a little a time, adding a little flour too if the mixture curdles, until the mixture is smooth and all the eggs have been incorporated. Stir in the remaining flour. Add the pears and their buttery juices, along with the thyme.

Spoon the mixture into the prepared pan and bake for about 40 minutes, until the cake has risen and is golden and springy.

Leave it to cool in the pan. Dust with sugar and cut into squares to serve.

For 1 Pot of Tea

3 teaspoons white tea
4–5 fresh kaffir lime leaves, lightly crushed
sugar or honey, to taste

Warm the teapot and the white tea and lime leaves. Fill the teapot with boiling water. Give everything a gentle stir and leave to infuse for 4–5 minutes. Sweeten to taste and pour into cups.

WHITE SWEET TEA (PAI MU TAN)
WITH CARDAMOM SHORTBREAD

Pai mu tan is a seriously delicious tea. Also known as White Peony, it comes from a variety of tea known as Narcissus or Chaicha, grown in the Fuijian province of China. A white tea, it is made from the unopened tea buds and the two earliest leaves to sprout, which are then left to wither and dry in the sun. It has a lovely naturally sweet, floral flavour and is one of my absolute favourites. Pai mu tan is a great tea to drink alone or alongside all manner of treats, but these delicately flavoured shortbreads somehow go so well – they make two graceful goodies together, I think.

120 g/1 stick soft butter
160 g/1¼ cups plain/
   all-purpose flour
60 g/⅓ cup caster/
   superfine sugar, plus
   extra for dusting
a pinch of salt
seeds from 5–6 cardamom
   pods, crushed

MAKES 20–24

Preheat the oven to 160°C (325°F) Gas 2.

Put all the ingredients in a large bowl and work until the mixture comes together to form a smooth dough. Shape it into a long sausage shape with a diameter of about 3 cm (7½ in), and wrap in clingfilm/plastic wrap. Refrigerate for about 30 minutes, until firm.

Cut the sausage into discs about 5 mm (1 in) thick and place on to non-stick cookie sheets, leaving space between each one for the shortbreads to spread.

Bake for about 15 minutes, until firm and golden. Cool on a wire rack, dust with sugar and store in an airtight container.

FOR 1 POT OF TEA

6 teaspoons Pai mu tan tea leaves
sugar or honey, to taste

Warm the teapot and add the leaves. Pour over water that has been boiled and slightly cooled. Leave to brew for 4–5 minutes. Sweeten to taste if necessary.

Fennel Tea
with Lemon and Almond Financiers

Financiers are delightful little cakes that are very similar to friands, but financiers are generally made with beurre noisette (butter that is heated to a lovely amber colour and an appealing nutty aroma). The name 'financier' is thought to come from the fact that they resemble bars of gold, or perhaps because they were popular in the cafés in the financial district of Paris. I love fennel tea, although it's not technically a tea, but an infusion. You can buy fennel tea bags or buy empty bags to create your own tea; simply whizz some fennel seeds up in a blender and add a tablespoon to each bag.

70 g/½ cup ground
  almonds/almond meal
30 g/¼ cup plain/
  all-purpose flour
a pinch of salt
120 g/1 generous cup
  icing/confectioners'
  sugar
grated zest of 2 lemons
100 g/6½ tablespoons
  butter
3 egg whites
50 g/½ cup flaked/slivered
  almonds

*6 mini loaf pans or small
  muffin moulds, lightly
  greased*

Makes 6

Preheat the oven to 180°C (350°F) Gas 4.

Mix the ground almonds/almond meal, flour, salt and sugar together in a large bowl. Stir in the lemon zest.

Melt the butter in a small saucepan and leave it over the heat until it turns to an amber colour and gives off a nutty aroma. Remove it from the heat and leave to cool slightly. Whisk the egg whites until frothy and light (you don't need to whip them to stiff peaks as you would if you were making meringues).

Trickle the butter into the dry ingredients and add half the egg whites. Mix lightly, and then add the remaining egg whites and continue to mix until fully incorporated.

Spoon the mixture into the prepared pans and scatter the flaked/slivered almonds over the top. Bake for about 15 minutes, until they are risen and golden and spring back when pressed lightly.

Serve warm, or leave to cool completely.

For 1 pot of tea
*2 fennel tea bags
sugar or honey, to taste*

Warm the pot and add the tea bags. Pour over boiling water and leave to infuse for about 5 minutes. Sweeten with sugar or honey and serve.

REFRESHINGLY DIFFERENT TEAS

I absolutely love the teas in this section – they really do show how deliciously different teas can be and how simple herbs and spices can make wonderful brews too. Sweet basil tea is such a delicate infusion, but one that is as surprising as it is sensational; the result of a very happy accident. Add treats such as white chocolate and redcurrant brownies, raspberry and clotted cream whirls, and Caribbean rum cake and you really will be on Cloud Nine.

Jasmine Flowering Tea
with Little Custard Tarts

Flowering tea never ceases to bring a huge smile to my face, and always elicits great excitement and intrigue when I serve it. The little flower bundles are made from dried tea leaves, which are wrapped and then tightly bound around one or more dried flower blossoms. When the boiling water is added, the bundle slowly unfurls to reveal the flower at the centre, and looks very beautiful. It's no gimmick either – they make lovely tea! Every bundle can be used up to three times without the tea becoming bitter or too weak, so if you're having friends for afternoon tea, or serving tea after a dinner party, all you need is a glass teapot or heatproof glass jug/pitcher, and you can watch the pretty spectacle unfold. Creamy, nutmeg-topped custard tarts encased in crisp, wafer-thin pastry are an elegant accompaniment to this very distinctive tea, and make afternoon cake-and-cuppa time very special indeed.

For the Pastry
175 g/1½ sticks soft butter
50 g/¼ cup caster/
   superfine sugar
1 egg yolk
250 g/2 cups plain/all-
   purpose flour, plus extra
   for dusting

For the Filling
2 egg yolks
2 whole eggs
250 ml/1 cup double/
   heavy cream
1 vanilla pod
50 g/¼ cup caster/
   superfine sugar
freshly grated nutmeg

*six 5-cm/2-in tartlet pans
   with removable base*

Makes 6

For the pastry, cream the butter and sugar together until light and fluffy. Stir in the egg yolk until fully combined. Lightly fold in the flour until a soft, smooth dough forms. Roll out on a lightly floured surface to a thickness of about 2 mm (⅛ in) and cut out six rounds about 6 cm (2½ in) in diameter. Line the tartlet pans, taking care to press the mixture into the corners. Refrigerate for 30 minutes.

Preheat the oven to 160°C (325°F) Gas 2. Beat the egg yolks, whole eggs and cream together until smooth. Split the vanilla pod lengthwise and scrape out the seeds. Stir the sugar and vanilla seeds into the eggs. Remove the tartlet cases from the fridge and place them on a baking sheet. Fill the cases with the custard mixture and grate a little fresh nutmeg over the top of each one. Bake for about 20 minutes, until the filling is set and golden. Leave to cool, then turn out of the pans and serve.

For 1 Pot of Tea
1 jasmine flowering tea bundle

Warm a glass teapot or heatproof glass jug/pitcher. Add the tea bundle and pour in very slightly cooled boiled water. In 2–3 minutes, the bundle will have unfurled and the tea will be ready to drink. Refill the pot up to three times.

Tea Slushes
with Salted Caramel and Blueberry Tart

Feather-light pastry, rich salted caramel, juicy blueberries and a glass of slushy semi-frozen, slightly sweet tea has to be pretty high up on the Absolute Bliss scale. Green or white tea are both great given the slush treatment, and my simple method involves freezing tea in ice cube moulds so you can make your cuppas as and when required! The tea is best very slightly sweetened because it's served frozen.

For the Pastry

175 g/1½ sticks soft butter
50 g/¼ cup caster/
    superfine sugar
a pinch of salt
1 egg yolk
250 g/2 cups plain/
    all-purpose flour, plus
    extra for dusting

For the Filling

397 g/14 oz. can sweetened
    condensed milk
150 g/¾ cup demerara
    sugar
50 g/3 tablespoons butter
100 ml/scant ½ cup
    double/heavy cream
½ teaspoon flaky sea salt,
    plus extra to garnish
50 g/1½ oz. dark chocolate
10 g/2 teaspoons butter
1 tablespoon golden syrup
    or light corn syrup
300 g/2 cups blueberries

*a 20-cm/8-in tart pan with
    removable base*

SERVES 6–8

Preheat the oven to 180°C (350°F) Gas 4.

Beat the butter, sugar and salt together until smooth. Add the egg yolk and stir until thoroughly combined. Fold in the flour and bring together to form a smooth dough. Wrap in clingfilm/plastic wrap and leave to rest in a cool place while preparing the filling.

For the filling, put the condensed milk, sugar and butter in a heavy-based saucepan over medium-low heat. Add the cream. Stir until the sugar has melted and the mixture is smooth. Increase the heat slightly and cook for 6–8 minutes, until thick and rich golden caramel in colour. Remove from the heat, add the salt and leave to cool. In the meantime, melt the chocolate, butter and golden syrup or corn syrup together. Leave to cool slightly.

Roll out the pastry on a lightly floured surface to fit the pan. Bake the pastry case blind for 10 minutes, until light golden and firm. Leave to cool.

Scatter the blueberries evenly over the base of the tart. Cover with an even layer of caramel. Trickle over the chocolate mixture and create swirls with a skewer. When the mixture is completely cold, sprinkle over another little pinch of salt flakes. Serve in slices.

For the Tea

*4 teaspoons green or white tea leaves
sugar or honey, to taste
mint leaves and lime slices, to garnish*

Brew the tea as usual, and sweeten very lightly. Pour into ice cube trays and freeze. To serve, place the cubes in a blender and blend to a slush. For a special touch, stir in some mint leaves and garnish with a slice of lime.

WHITE TEA PEARLS
WITH RASPBERRY AND CLOTTED CREAM WHIRLS

White tea pearls are lovely, and make an exquisite cup of tea. The leaves are carefully rolled into pearls and left to dry in the sun. When steeped, they unravel, releasing their lovely, fresh flavour and all those precious antioxidants. A special tea deserves a special accompaniment, and these buttery crisp whirls filled with clotted cream and raspberries fit the bill wonderfully.

250 g/2 sticks soft butter

200 g/1⅔ cups plain/all-purpose flour

50 g/½ cup cornflour/cornstarch

50 g/scant ½ cup icing/confectioners' sugar

1 teaspoon pure vanilla extract

FOR THE FILLING

300 g/1¼ cups clotted cream

250 g/2 cups raspberries

caster/granulated sugar, for dusting

2 baking sheets, lined with baking parchment

a piping/pastry bag with a star nozzle/tip

MAKES ABOUT 10

Preheat the oven to 180°C (350°F) Gas 4.

Mix the butter, flours, icing/confectioners' sugar and pure vanilla extract together until it forms a smooth dough. Spoon the mixture into a piping/pastry bag and pipe oval shapes about the size of a large egg onto the prepared baking sheets. Bake for about 15 minutes, until golden. Remove from the oven and leave to cool for a few minutes, then transfer to a wire rack until completely cold.

To serve, sandwich together with clotted cream and raspberries and dust lightly with sugar.

FOR 1 POT OF TEA

3 teaspoons white tea pearls
sugar or honey, to taste

Warm the teapot and add the white tea pearls. Pour over boiled water that has cooled slightly. Brew for 4–5 minutes. Sweeten with sugar or honey. This is a lovely, delicate tea, so adding milk isn't really a good idea.

Bubble Tea (Zhen Zhu)
with Sesame Sandcakes

Pearl milk tea, zhen zhu or, as it is mostly referred to, bubble tea, has become something of a trendy drink in recent years, with bubble teashops popping up in major cities around the world. It is instantly recognizable by the super-sized balls of tapioca that sit at the bottom of a glass of fruit- or milk-based iced tea. Traditionally, bubble tea was a simple concoction, made with ordinary tapioca pearls and sweetened with evaporated or condensed milk. The accompanying sandcakes are crunchy and loaded with sesame seeds, but not over-sweet.

100 g/6⅓ tablespoons soft
   butter
75 g/⅓ cup caster/
   superfine sugar
a pinch of salt
150 g/1 cup plus
   2 tablespoon plain/
   all-purpose flour
50 g/scant ½ cup ground
   almonds/almond meal
5 tablespoons sesame
   seeds

Makes about 20

Preheat the oven to 180°C (350°F) Gas 4.

Cream the butter, sugar and salt together until smooth. Add the flour, almonds and sesame seeds and mix until everything is fully combined and the mixture is smooth.

Place tablespoons of the mixture onto a non-stick baking sheet, allowing a little room in between them so that the cookies can spread. Bake in the oven for about 10 minutes, until golden. Remove from the oven and allow to cool for 5 minutes. Transfer to a wire rack and allow to cool completely before storing in an airtight container.

For the Tea

4 tablespoons tapioca pearls
2 teaspoons caster/granulated sugar
4 cups green or black tea, refrigerated
3 tablespoons sweetened condensed milk, or to taste

Place the tapioca pearls in a saucepan. Cover with about 600 ml (2½ cups) cold water and cook for about 20 minutes, until the tapioca is soft but not overcooked. Drain and rinse under cold water. Transfer to a bowl and stir in the sugar. Put a spoonful or so of the tapioca pearls into each of 4 glasses, followed by a few ice cubes. Pour in enough tea to come three-quarters of the way up the glasses. Stir in the condensed milk to taste and serve.

Sweet Basil Tea
with white chocolate and redcurrant brownies

Basil is associated with all things Italian, and usually savoury. But I had a notion one day that the leaves might make an interesting infusion, and my instinct paid off, because I fell in love with this lovely tisane. These white chocolate and redcurrant brownies seem to be a big hit with everyone who tries them. The white chocolate gives them a delicious flavour, and the almonds add a lovely soft, dense texture without them being heavy. I think this is a combination you'll be delighted you tried.

250 g/2 sticks butter

400 g/2 cups caster/
   superfine sugar

200 g/7 oz. white chocolate

4 eggs, beaten

200 g/1⅔ cups ground
   almonds/almond meal

100 g/¾ cup plain/
   all-purpose flour

1 teaspoon baking powder

100 g/⅔ cup redcurrants

icing/confectioners' sugar,
   for dusting

*a 23-cm/9-in square cake
   pan, greased and lined
   with baking parchment*

Makes 36

Preheat the oven to 180°C (350°F) Gas 4.

Put the butter, sugar and white chocolate in a microwave-proof bowl and microwave at medium-high for 1 minute. Stir and return the mixture to the microwave for a further 30 seconds, until fully melted. Leave to cool slightly, then stir in the beaten eggs.

Add the almonds, flour, baking powder and redcurrants, and mix well. Pour the mixture into the prepared pan. Bake for about 30 minutes, until firm and golden. Leave to cool, then cut into bite-size squares. Dust with icing/confectioners' sugar and serve.

For 1 pot of tea

3–4 handfuls fresh basil leaves
2 teaspoons sugar, or to taste

Put the basil leaves and sugar in the pot and pour in the water. Stir gently and leave to infuse for 3–4 minutes. Pour into cups and add more sugar to taste, as desired. It needs a little sugar to bring out the delicate flavours; start with a very small amount and adjust accordingly.

CINNAMON-SCENTED BLACK TEA
WITH CARIBBEAN RUM CAKE

The main difference between black tea and other types is the greater oxidation of the leaves; this means that black teas hold their flavour for much longer, and are often mixed with strong spices and flavourings. Here, I've used a robust black tea and infused it with a cinnamon stick. This glorious rum-soaked cake will accompany your slightly spiced cuppa perfectly.

250 g/2 sticks soft butter

250 g/1¼ cups caster/
    superfine sugar

4 eggs, beaten

250 g/2¼ cups ground
    almonds/almond meal

100 g/¾ cup plain/all-
    purpose flour

2 teaspoons baking powder

90 ml/6 tablespoons
    good-quality dark
    Caribbean rum

FOR THE SYRUP

100 g/½ cup caster/
    granulated sugar

50 ml/3 tablespoons good-
    quality dark Caribbean
    rum

*a 24-cm/9½-in ring-shaped
    cake pan, greased*

MAKES 10–12 SLICES

Preheat the oven to 180°C (350°F) Gas 4.

Beat the butter and sugar together until light and fluffy. Add the eggs a little at a time until fully incorporated. Stir in the almonds, flour and baking powder and mix until smooth. Beat in the rum.

Spoon the mixture into the prepared pan and bake for about 1 hour, until it is risen and is golden and springs back when pressed lightly in the centre. Leave to cool in the pan for about 10–15 minutes.

In the meantime, put 100 ml (⅓ cup) water, the sugar and rum in a saucepan and heat until the sugar is melted. Bubble for 1–2 minutes until the mixture is slightly syrupy, then remove from the heat.

Turn the cake out of the pan and place on a wire rack set over a plate. Make pin pricks in the surface of the cake and spoon the syrup over until fully soaked into the cake. Any syrup that runs through will be caught on the plate and can be re-applied. Leave to cool completely before serving.

FOR THE TEA

black tea leaves (I love Yunnan)
cinnamon sticks
sugar or honey, to taste

Take a scoop of black tea in a tea ball and place in a tall mug with a cinnamon stick. Pour over boiled water and leave to infuse. Sweeten with the tiniest amount of sugar or honey, which helps balance the cinnamon flavour.

Ginger Tea
WITH STICKY MOLASSES AND PUMPKIN CAKE

This is definitely one for gingerholics. If you need to sweeten the tea, I think honey is a better choice in this instance, as it will add another dimension to the duo.

320 g/2½ cups plain/
    all-purpose flour
1 teaspoon bicarbonate
    of soda/baking soda
1½ teaspoons ground
    ginger
200 g/1 cup dark molasses/
    turbinado sugar
100 ml/scant ⅓ cup golden
    syrup
100 g/6½ tablespoons
    butter, melted
3 eggs, beaten
150 g/⅔ cup cooked
    pumpkin, puréed
    (or use canned)
120 g/4 oz. stem/candied
    ginger, roughly chopped
butter, to serve

a 900-g/2-lb. loaf pan,
lightly greased and lined
with baking parchment

MAKES 10-12 SLICES

Preheat the oven to 180°C (350°F) Gas 4.

Put the flour, bicarbonate of soda/baking soda and ground ginger in a large bowl. Stir in the molasses/turbinado sugar.

In a separate bowl, beat the golden syrup, melted butter, eggs and pumpkin purée together until smooth. Stir into the dry ingredients and mix until everything is fully incorporated. Stir in the chopped stem/candied ginger.

Spoon the mixture into the prepared pan and bake for about 1¼ hours, or until the loaf is risen and golden and a skewer inserted into the centre comes out clean.

Leave the cake to cool in the pan for about 15 minutes, then turn onto a wire rack to cool completely. Serve with butter.

FOR 1 POT OF TEA
3 heaped teaspoons green tea leaves
1½-cm/¾-in piece fresh ginger, sliced
honey, to taste

Warm the teapot, add the leaves and ginger and pour over boiled water. Brew for 5 minutes. Sweeten as desired.

JAPANESE MATCHA TEA
WITH CHOCOLATE SUSHI ROLLS

Matcha is a green tea most commonly found in powdered form, and is unique to Japan; for hundreds of years it has traditionally been the basis for the Japanese tea ceremony. It has a complex and acquired taste: initially astringent with a lingering, sweeter finish. Making matcha tea involves mixing the powder to a paste with a special tea scoop, then thinning it to the required consistency with warm water and a small bamboo whisk. You can buy the powder in kit form along with Japanese tea cups, scoops and whisks, and the powder crops up in trendy recipes to flavour and colour both savoury and sweet dishes – so it's well worth experimenting with, if you're so inclined! The chocolate sushi is great fun – they look and taste amazing, but it's important to temper the chocolate to give it a lovely, glossy shine. Don't worry, though: tempering chocolate doesn't have to be all scraping and spreading and cold marble. 'Seeded' tempering is a doddle, and all you need is a digital thermometer, which is a great asset in the kitchen anyway. In warmer weather, when chocolate work may be more difficult, you can also substitute the tempered chocolate for blackberry fruit leather (as pictured).

250 g/1¼ cups sushi rice
250 ml/1 cup coconut milk
60 g/⅓ cup caster/
    granulated sugar
generous ½ teaspoon salt
finely grated zest of
    1 lemon
200 g/6½ oz. good-quality
    dark chocolate (about
    70%)
½ ripe mango, peeled and
    cut into julienne strips

a digital thermometer

*2 baking sheets, lined with
    baking parchment*

MAKES 10-12 ROLLS

Put the sushi rice in a saucepan and add 300 ml (1¼ cups) water and 200 ml (¾ cup) of the coconut milk. Bring to the boil, then reduce the heat and simmer for 15 minutes, stirring to prevent sticking. Turn off the heat and cover the pan. Leave to stand for 15 minutes, without removing the lid; the rice will continue to cook. Stir in the remaining coconut milk, sugar, salt and lemon zest. Leave to cool completely.

Break the chocolate into pieces. Place half of it in a heatproof bowl and set it over a pan of barely simmering water. Heat until the chocolate has melted and reaches 46°C (115°F). Remove the bowl from the heat. Add the remaining chocolate, a square or two at a time, and stir until it has melted and the temperature comes down to 32°C (90°F). Spread half the chocolate on one of the prepared baking sheets in an 8 x 20-cm (3¼ x 8-inch) rectangle. Repeat to make another rectangle on the other tray. Leave in a cool place (but do not refrigerate) until the chocolate has set but is still pliable.

Leaving a gap of about 1 cm (½ in) from the bottom edge of the chocolate, spread half the rice mixture in a band about 5–6 cm (2–2½ in) deep across the length of the chocolate. Gently lay the mango pieces across the centre of the rice, as if you were making nori sushi. Take the edge of the baking parchment closest to you and carefully but firmly roll the chocolate and rice, again as if you were making ordinary sushi. Press the ends together firmly and hold there for a minute or two: the warmth of your hands should seal the chocolate. Cut into pieces about 5 cm (2 in) long.

Repeat with the remaining chocolate and rice and serve immediately.

FOR THE TEA

8 teaspoons matcha tea powder

Put the tea in a jug/pitcher. Using a wire whisk, mix to a paste. Gradually add warm water and whisk quickly in a figure-of-eight motion until frothy. Pour into small cups and serve.

MASALA CHAI WITH PEANUT CHIKKI

A favourite tea in India, masala chai is growing in popularity and can be bought ready-spiced in many forms, but is easily made at home, too. It is usually made with a black tea base that is boiled with sugar and milk, along with spices such as cardamom, cinnamon and ginger to create a thick, syrupy drink that is lovely at any time of day. I've paired it with another Indian treat, crunchy peanut chikki, a close relative of peanut brittle. I'm not too sure what my dentist would make of the combination, but once in a while naughty-but-nice just has to be done! I have a lovely shop-bought chai masala that I enjoy, which is a fragrant concoction of black tea, cinnamon, allspice, ginger, ginseng, red peppercorns and cardamom, but I've included a recipe here that was given to me by my lovely friends Nioshka and Blaise. It is much more fun to make your own – authentically Indian and delicious to boot!

150 g/¾ cup caster/ granulated sugar
150 g/1 cup roasted, lightly salted peanuts

a sugar thermometer

a baking sheet, lightly greased

SERVES 8–10

Put the sugar and 100 ml (⅓ cup) water in a heavy-based saucepan over low heat and cook until the sugar has completely dissolved. Use a lightly dampened pastry brush to wash down the side of the saucepan. Do not stir.

Once the sugar has dissolved, increase the heat and let the mixture bubble until it develops a dark amber colour and reaches a temperature of 154°C (309°F) on a sugar thermometer. Carefully stir in the peanuts, then immediately tip the mixture onto the prepared baking sheet, taking great care as the mixture is dangerously hot. Leave to cool completely, then break into shards. Store in an airtight container.

FOR THE TEA

3–4 teaspoons black tea
1 cm/½ in fresh ginger, sliced
2–3 green cardamom pods

100 ml/⅓ cup milk
sugar, to taste

Blaise categorically refers to this as a 'brew' and says that you could add milk to the cup, but it's much better added to the brew! It's a lovely, subtle tea – not overpoweringly spicy as I've found some bought varieties to be. Thank you, Blaise! Pour 1 litre (4 cups) water into a saucepan and bring to the boil. Add the tea leaves, ginger and cardamom. Bubble for 3–4 minutes. Add the milk, bring back to the boil and remove from the heat. Add sugar to taste.

Mint and Summer Berry Iced Tea
with Strawberry and Rosewater Cream Meringues

4 egg whites
200 g/1 cup caster/
   superfine sugar
1–2 drops pink food
   colouring or grenadine

For the filling

300 ml/1¼ cups
   double/heavy cream
2 teaspoons caster/
   granulated sugar
2 teaspoons rosewater
250 g/1 pint strawberries,
   quartered

To decorate

white and pink rose petals
1 egg white, beaten
2 tablespoons caster/
   granulated sugar

*2 baking sheets, lined with
   baking parchment*

an electric hand whisk

*a piping/pastry bag
   (optional)*

Makes 8–10

This is a lovely summer tisane, and not technically a true tea, although you could add green tea to the pot if you wish. Vary the berries according to what's available, but a mixture looks pretty. Don't be too heavy-handed with the sweetening, as the meringues are deliciously and indulgently sweet! Be sure to use unsprayed roses.

Preheat the oven to 150°C (300°F) Gas 2.

Whisk the egg whites in a scrupulously clean bowl until firm (unless you're training for the Olympics, an electric hand whisk is probably best for this). Add the sugar about a tablespoon at a time, and keep whisking until all the sugar has been incorporated. Gently fold in the food colouring.

Using two spoons (or a piping/pastry bag if preferred), place small dollops on the prepared baking sheets, spaced a little way apart. Bake for about 20 minutes, then switch off the oven. Leave the meringues in the oven until cold.

In the meantime, whisk the cream, sugar and rosewater together, until the cream has thickened. Dip the rose petals lightly into the egg white, then gently into the sugar to coat. Leave to dry.

Sandwich the meringues together with the cream and strawberries and pile them onto a serving platter. Scatter over the rose petals and serve.

For 1 pot of tea

*1 large bunch fresh mint,
   plus extra to serve*
caster/granulated sugar, to taste

ice cubes, to serve
*250 g/9 oz. mixed summer
   berries*

Put the mint in a teapot and pour over boiling water. Muddle the leaves (as if you were making a mojito) and leave to cool and infuse. Pour into a glass jug/pitcher and refrigerate until very cold. Remove the leaves and pour into 4 tall glasses. Add ice cubes, summer berries and mint leaves and serve with straws.

LEMONGRASS TEA
WITH PISTACHIO AND ALMOND BAKLAVA

Sticky-sweet baklava make a great treat for anyone with a sweet tooth. Often paired with strong coffee, they taste divine with a gently perfumed cup of lemongrass tea, too. When you have poured the first cup, repeat the brewing process – there should still be enough flavour to produce a second cup. I love this as it is, but those with a sweet tooth could add a little honey. Sometimes I use white or green tea as a base, but the lemongrass alone makes a very special tea.

300 g/2 cups pistachio
  nuts, roughly chopped
50 g/scant ½ cup ground
  almonds/almond meal
2 teaspoons ground
  cinnamon
200 g/6½ oz. filo/phyllo
  pastry dough
150 g/1 stick plus
  2 tablespoons butter,
  melted
grated zest and juice
  of 2 large oranges
juice of 1 lemon
200 g/1 cup caster/
  granulated sugar
seeds from 2 cardamom
  pods
seeds from 1 vanilla pod

*an 18 x 30-cm/7 x 12-in
  roasting pan or
  rectangular cake pan,
  lightly greased*

MAKES 16

Preheat the oven to 180°C (350°F) Gas 4.

Mix the pistachios, almonds and cinnamon together and set aside.

Layer half the filo/phyllo pastry in the pan, brushing each sheet with melted butter as you go. Scatter the nuts evenly over the pastry. Cover with the remaining pastry, brushing each sheet with melted butter as before. Brush the top with melted butter and tuck the edges of the pastry in around the edges. Carefully cut a diamond pattern into the pastry.

Bake for 20 minutes, then reduce the oven temperature to 150°C (300°F) Gas 2. Bake for a further 10–15 minutes or so, until crisp and golden.

Meanwhile, place the orange juice and zest, lemon juice, sugar, cardamom, vanilla seeds and pod and 200 ml (¾ cup) water in a saucepan and heat until the sugar has melted. Bubble for 3–4 minutes, until the mixture is slightly syrupy. Leave to cool.

Remove the baklava from the oven. Remove the vanilla pod from the syrup and pour the syrup evenly over the baklava. Leave for several hours and allow the syrup to soak into the pastry. Cut into diamonds and serve.

FOR 1 POT OF TEA

4–5 long stems lemongrass
floral honey, to taste

Give the lemongrass stems a good bash with a rolling pin and cut them into slices about 5 mm (¼ inch) thick. Place them in a teapot and fill with boiling water. Stir well and leave to infuse for 3–4 minutes. Pour into cups and sweeten with floral honey, if desired.

TI KUAN YIN TEA WITH EGYPTIAN BASBOUSA

This is a very unusual but no less lovely combination: dense, sticky Egyptian basbousa and a slightly smoky, nutty oolong tea that is one of China's most appreciated. Ti kuan yin comes from the Fujian province and is also called Tie guan yin, which means 'Iron Goddess of Mercy'. The first time I tried it, I was puzzled by its distinctive smell and found it hard to pinpoint just what it reminded me of. Later, when researching suppliers, I read a description saying the tea has notes of toasted walnut and kale/collard greens – and the penny dropped! Please don't let that put you off, though, as it really is a delicious tea and makes a great partner for the sticky-sweet diamonds that are Arabic basbousa. I've made my basbousa slightly less sweet than the traditional version, but unless you have a remarkably sweet tooth, I'm sure you'll still find it sweet and sticky enough!

FOR THE BASBOUSA
225 ml/scant 1 cup full-fat
   plain yoghurt
150 g/1⅓ cups ground
   almonds/almond meal
185 g/1½ sticks butter,
   melted
225 g/1 cup plus
   2 tablespoons caster/
   granulated sugar
300 g/2¼ cups semolina
a pinch of salt
1½ teaspoons baking
   powder
finely grated zest of
   1 lemon

FOR THE SYRUP
150 g/¾ cup caster/
   granulated sugar
juice of 1 lemon

*a 20 x 30-cm/8 x 12-in
   rectangular roasting dish
   or cake pan, lightly greased*

MAKES 16

Preheat the oven to 180°C (350°F) Gas 4.

Put all the ingredients for the basbousa in a large bowl and beat until smooth. Pour the mixture into the prepared pan and bake for about 30 minutes, until golden and set.

In the meantime, put the sugar, 100 ml (⅓ cup) water and lemon juice in a saucepan and heat until the sugar has melted. Bubble for 4–5 minutes until thick and syrupy. Remove from the heat and leave to cool.

Remove the cake from the oven and pour the cold syrup evenly over the top. Return to the oven for a couple of minutes.

Cut into diamonds and serve.

FOR 1 POT OF TEA
*2–3 tablespoons Ti kuan yin leaves
sugar or honey, to taste*

Warm the teapot and add the leaves. Add slightly cooled boiled water and leave to brew for 4–5 minutes. Sweeten with sugar or honey as desired.

Gyokuro Tea
WITH FUDGY DARK CHOCOLATE AND ALMOND CAKES

Gyokuro tea is one of Japan's finest teas. The leaves have a higher concentration of chlorophyll, which give them a vivid green colour and a sweet, pronounced flavour. They are steamed to prevent oxidization. It's important to allow the boiled water to cool before brewing, or the delicate flavour will be compromised. Dark, fudgy chocolate cake makes a really superb combination with this impressive tea.

250 g/2 sticks soft butter
350 g/1¾ cups caster/
   superfine sugar
6 eggs, beaten
150 g/1 cup plus
   2 tablespoons plain/
   all-purpose flour
150 g/1⅓ cups ground
   almonds/almond meal
1 teaspoon almond essence

FOR THE FUDGE TOPPING,
180 g/scant 1 cup
   caster/granulated sugar
100 g/6½ tablespoons
   butter
250 g/8 oz. dark chocolate
150 ml/⅔ cup evaporated
   milk

*a 20 x 30-cm/8 x 12-in deep
   roasting pan or cake pan,
   lightly greased*

MAKES 15

Preheat the oven to 180°C (350°F) Gas 4.

Beat the butter and sugar together until light and fluffy. Add the eggs a little at a time until the mixture is smooth (you may have to add a little flour in between each addition to prevent curdling). Stir in the remaining flour, almonds and almond essence. Spoon into the prepared pan and bake for about 50 minutes, until risen and golden. Leave to cool in the pan.

In the meantime, make the fudge topping. Place all the ingredients into a saucepan and heat until the sugar has dissolved and the butter and chocolate have melted. Simmer over gentle heat for 3–4 minutes, until the mixture thickens. Beat for 2–3 minutes until glossy, then refrigerate until cold.

Spread the filling over the cold cake. Cut into squares and serve.

FOR 1 POT OF TEA

4–5 teaspoons Gyokuro tea leaves
sugar or honey, to taste

Warm the pot and add the tea leaves. Boil the water and leave it to cool to about 60°C (140°F), then pour it over the tea leaves. Brew for 3–4 minutes. It can be steeped again a couple of times, but the subsequent brewing times should be shorter.

AFTERNOON TEAS

Taking time out in the afternoon to enjoy a pot of tea and a sweet treat should be something we do much more often. It's definitely a good time for sharing something special to eat with the people we care about, without the formality of having to prepare a full meal. Whether it's a full-flavoured gunpowder tea with a slice of sticky walnut tart enjoyed by the fire on a cold winter's day, or an al fresco indulgence of lime iced tea with pretty borage flower ice cubes and irresistible cherry and blueberry eccles cakes in the summer. It's the tea and cake equivalents of chicken soup for the soul.

Lime Iced Tea with Borage Ice Cubes
and Cherry and Blueberry Eccles Cakes

White tea complements the refreshing flavour of fresh lime in this lovely summer infusion. Borage-flower ice cubes are wonderful to keep in the freezer: add them to ice teas, cold drinks and cocktails for a special touch. Traditional Eccles cakes were always a favourite in my house – my mum made the best ones!

500 g/1 lb. pitted/stoned cherries

1 teaspoon arrowroot

120 g/⅔ cup caster/granulated
  sugar

150 g/1 cup blueberries

425 g/15 oz. ready-rolled puff
  pastry dough

Makes 8

Preheat the oven to 200°C (400°F) Gas 6.

Put the cherries in a saucepan with 3 tablespoons water. Cook over gentle heat until the juices ooze. Mix the arrowroot with 4 tablespoons cold water and add this to the cherries, stirring all the time, so that the mixture thickens without becoming lumpy. Add 100 g (½ cup) of the sugar and cook for 2–3 minutes. Stir in the blueberries and leave to cool.

Meanwhile, cut eight 6-cm (2½-in) rounds from the puff pastry. Put a small spoonful of the fruit in the centre of each round. Moisten the edges with water and gather the pastry up and around the filling. Crimp the edges together firmly to seal them, then gently turn it over so the seam is on the bottom. Repeat with the other pastry circles and arrange on a baking sheet.

Brush the surface of each cake with water, and then dust with the remaining sugar. Bake for about 15 minutes, until golden. Serve slightly warm or cold.

For 1 Pot of Tea

4 bags white tea
  (or use fresh leaves)
3 limes, thinly sliced
fresh mint leaves, to serve
honey or caster sugar, to taste

For the Ice Cubes

a handful of borage flowers
an ice cube tray

Several hours beforehand, put the borage flowers in ice cube trays, fill with water and freeze. Warm a teapot. Add the tea and 2 of the limes and fill with boiling water. Brew for 4–5 minutes. Pour into tea glasses, add an extra slice of lime and some mint leaves, and sweeten if desired.

WHITE TEA
WITH BUTTERY CARROT AND ORANGE CAKE

Life beyond builders' tea has truly been one of the most amazing discoveries I have made in recent years, but sometimes – when I'm in a hurry or a little preoccupied, and I just need to stick a tea bag in a cup – the box of white tea bags I keep in the cupboard is a godsend. I like the Twinings white tea bags, which make an elegant, quite delicate, very drinkable cuppa, but there are lots of other nice brands out there. Carrot cake is always a favourite; this one is made with butter, and has a lovely flavour and lightness. I've topped it with sweetened mascarpone, which I find is less cloying than the traditional cream cheese frosting. I've also used orange zest to decorate, although sometimes I make little baby carrots out of coloured marzipan or fondant icing.

250 g/2 sticks soft butter

250 g/1¼ cups golden caster/granulated sugar, plus extra for dusting

4 eggs, beaten

300 g/2⅓ cups self-raising/rising flour

2 large carrots, peeled and grated

2 teaspoons ground cinnamon

grated zest and juice of 1 orange

50 g/⅓ cup sultanas/golden raisins

FOR THE TOPPING,

50 g/3 tablespoons mascarpone

100 g/½ cup caster/superfine sugar

zest of 2 oranges, cut into fine slivers or shavings

a 20 x 30-cm/8 x 12-in cake pan, greased

MAKES 15

Preheat the oven to 180°C (350°F) Gas 4.

Cream the butter and sugar together until light and fluffy. Beat in the eggs a little at a time, until the mixture is smooth. You can add a little flour in between each addition if the mixture seems to be curdling.

Stir in the remaining flour, grated carrot, cinnamon and orange juice and zest. Add the sultanas/golden raisins and stir until everything is fully incorporated. Spoon the mixture into the prepared pan and bake for 35–40 minutes, until risen and golden. Dust with a little more sugar and leave to cool in the pan.

To make the topping, beat the mascarpone and sugar together. Cut the cake into squares and decorate with little dollops of the mascarpone mixture and a little orange zest.

FOR 1 POT OF TEA

3 white tea bags

Warm the pot and add the tea. Pour over water that has been boiled and cooled very slightly. Leave to infuse for 5 minutes before serving.

FOR THe BASe
200 g/1¾ sticks butter
200 g/1⅔ cups plain/
  all-purpose flour
100 g/¾ cup rice flour
100 g/½ cup caster/
  superfine sugar

FOR THe TOPPING
600 ml/2½ cups
  double/heavy cream
300 g/1½ cups caster/
  superfine sugar, plus
  extra for dusting
4 eggs, beaten
100 g/¾ cup plain/
  all-purpose flour
grated zest and juice
  of 4 large lemons

*a deep 20 x 25-cm/8 x 10-in
  roasting pan or cake pan,
  greased and lined with
  baking parchment*

MAKeS 15

Pu-erh tea is a fermented dark tea from Yunnan province in China. It goes back hundreds of years, and was once an everyday, affordable tea, but is now relatively expensive. It's a very pleasant tea with a distinctive aroma, and has a reputation for aiding weight loss. Not so much for me, maybe because I like to drink it with these irresistible lemon fudge slices…

Preheat the oven to 180°C (350°F) Gas 4.

For the base, rub the butter, flour and rice flour together until the mixture resembles fine breadcrumbs. Add the sugar and bring it together to form a smooth dough. Push the mixture into the prepared pan in an even layer and smooth with the back of a spoon. Bake for about 15 minutes, until firm and golden.

In the meantime, make the topping. Whisk the cream, sugar and eggs together. Slowly add the flour and whisk until smooth. Add the lemon zest and juice.

Remove the cooked base from the oven and immediately pour on the lemon mixture. Return to the oven and bake for a further 20–25 minutes, until the topping is set. Remove from the oven and leave to cool completely. Dust lightly with sugar and cut into bars.

FOR 1 POT OF Tea
*3-4 teaspoons pu-erh tea leaves
sugar or honey, to taste*

Warm the pot and add the tea leaves. Pour over boiled, slightly cooled water and leave to brew for 4–5 minutes. Sweeten to taste with sugar or honey.

Autumn Tea
with Best-ever Chocolate Brownies

The best tea companies all have their own special blends, but teas designed for particular times of year, such as summer, autumn/fall and Christmas are very popular. I particularly like the teas of Betjeman & Barton – they have a lovely autumn/fall blend that contains dried pieces of quince, figs, raisins and hazelnuts. When the days are cooler and shorter, it's nice to have a tea that has a little extra 'oomph', something that makes you feel you have all the flavours of autumn/fall in your cup. These flavoured teas are generally based on black tea because the stronger flavour of the tea can handle the warmer spices. The brownies are addictive. The great thing is they don't contain any flour, so they're gluten free, but still taste incredible. Try them – I think you'll love them!

250 g/2 sticks butter
400 g/2 cups caster/
   superfine sugar
120 g/4 oz. dark chocolate
   (64–72%), broken into
   pieces
50 g/½ cup cocoa powder
4 eggs, beaten
300 g/2⅓ cups ground
   almonds/almond meal
fresh raspberries, to serve

a 20 x 30-cm/8 x 12-in
   roasting pan or cake pan,
   lightly greased and lined
   with baking parchment

Makes 15

Preheat the oven to 180°C (350°F) Gas 4.

Put the butter, sugar, chocolate and cocoa powder in a large heatproof bowl and set it over a pan of gently simmering water. Leave until the butter and chocolate have melted. Give the mixture a good stir – it should be nice and smooth.

Remove from the heat, let it cool slightly and stir in the eggs. Add the almonds and stir until everything is fully incorporated and the mixture is smooth and glossy. Pour the mixture into the prepared pan and bake for 35–40 minutes, until springy to the touch. Leave to cool in the pan, then cut into squares.

For 1 pot of tea
4 teaspoons autumn/fall blend tea
sugar and milk, to taste

Warm the teapot and add the tea. Pour on simmering water and let stand for 3–4 minutes. Add milk and sugar, as desired.

Tregothnan Estate Tea
with Hazelnut, Peach and Redcurrant Frangipane Tart

Hidden away on the banks of the River Fal in Cornwall lies the Tregothnan Estate, the family home of Lord Falmouth since 1335. For centuries, Tregothnan's astounding micro-climate has supported many extraordinary species of fruit trees and an enormous range of rare plants. In recent years it has been producing the very first English teas, and they are fast gaining fans – as far away as China and beyond! Hazelnut makes a lovely frangipane-style base for this peach and redcurrant-topped tart, although you could easily vary the fruit according to season.

For the Pastry
175 g/1½ sticks butter
50 g/¼ cup caster/
  superfine sugar
a pinch of salt
1 egg yolk
250 g/2 cups plain/
  all-purpose flour, plus
  extra for dusting

For the Filling
200 g/1¾ sticks soft butter
200 g/1⅓ cups toasted
  hazelnuts, finely
  chopped
200 g/1 cup caster/
  superfine sugar
a pinch of salt
2 eggs
6 ripe peaches
150 g/generous 1 cup
  redcurrants
100 ml/6 tablespoons
  apricot jam/jelly, sieved

*a 23-cm/9-in tart pan with
  removable base*

Serves 8

Preheat the oven to 170°C (325°F) Gas 3.

Beat the butter, sugar and salt together until smooth. Add the egg yolk and stir until thoroughly combined. Fold in the flour and bring the mixture together to form a smooth dough. Wrap in clingfilm/plastic wrap and leave to rest in a cool place while preparing the filling.

Beat the butter, hazelnuts, sugar, salt and eggs together until smooth.

Roll the pastry out on a lightly floured surface and use it to line the tart pan. Spoon the hazelnut filling evenly into the base. Bake for about 30 minutes, until the filling is firm in the centre.

Cut the peaches in half, remove the stone/pit and cut each one into 8 slices. Arrange over the top of tart in slightly overlapping concentric circles, starting at the outside edge. Scatter over the redcurrants. Warm the apricot jam/jelly slightly and stir in 1 tablespoon hot water. Brush it carefully over the top to glaze. Leave to cool and serve in slices.

For 1 Pot of Tea
*3–4 teaspoons Tregothnan Estate tea
sugar or honey, to taste*

Warm the pot and add the tea. Pour over boiling water and leave to brew for 3–4 minutes. Sweeten with sugar or honey, as desired.

LADY GREY TEA WITH RASPBERRY MACARONS

*Lady Grey tea is related to the celebrated Earl Grey; it is also a black tea scented
with oil of bergamot, but has less bergamot, and also contains lemon and orange oils.
It was named in honour of Mary Elizabeth Grey, the wife of the original Earl Grey.
Sadly though, romantic notions of Mary Elizabeth sliding effortlessly into the drawing
room to sip her namesake tea are misplaced – it was invented in the 1990s! I'm sure that
if Lady Mary Elizabeth had been around, she would have given the nod of approval,
though, especially if her tea was served alongside these moreish raspberry macarons.*

220 g/1¼ cups icing/
   confectioners' sugar
160 g/1⅓ cups ground
   almonds/almond meal
4 large egg whites
a pinch of salt
95 g/½ cup caster/
   superfine sugar
red food colouring gel
200 g/¾ cup high fruit-
   content raspberry
   jam/jelly

a food processor

*2 or 3 baking sheets, lined
   with baking parchment*

a piping/pastry bag

Makes about 30

Draw 4-cm (1½-inch) circles (spaced a little apart) on the baking parchment as templates so that all the macarons come out the same size; they'll look much prettier when finished.

Blitz the icing/confectioners' sugar and almonds in a food processor until very fine, then push the mixture through a fine-meshed sieve. Set aside.

Whisk the egg whites and salt together until stiff and glossy. Add the sugar, about a third at a time, beating again each time, until the eggs are stiff and glossy and all the sugar has been incorporated.

Carefully but thoroughly fold the almond mixture into the egg whites, until fully incorporated but still light. Fold in enough food colouring to achieve the desired pink colour. Spoon the mixture into a large piping/pastry bag and pipe circles onto the parchment, following the circles you drew earlier.

When all the macarons have been piped, take hold of the baking sheet and tap it firmly on the work surface 2 or 3 times to knock out any air bubbles. Preheat the oven to 140°C (275°F) Gas ½ and leave the baking sheets to stand for 30 minutes.

Bake the macarons for about 15 minutes, until the shells are crisp and they have grown little 'feet'. Remove from the oven and leave to cool. Once completely cool, sandwich with the raspberry jam/jelly and serve.

For 1 pot of tea
5 teaspoons Lady Grey tea

Warm the teapot and add the tea. Pour in boiling water and leave to brew for 5 minutes or so. Serve with lemon.

FOR THE PASTRY

175 g/1½ sticks soft butter

50 g/¼ cup caster/
    superfine sugar

a pinch of salt

1 egg yolk

250 g/2 cups plain/
    all-purpose flour, plus
    extra for dusting

FOR THE FILLING

50 g/3 tablespoons butter

100 g/½ cup soft brown
    sugar

100 g/scant ½ cup set honey

a pinch of salt

150 ml/⅔ cup double/
    heavy cream

2 eggs, beaten

225 g/1½ cups walnut pieces

*a 23-cm/9-in tart pan with
    removable base*

SERVES 6–8

GUNPOWDER TEA WITH WALNUT TART

Preheat the oven to 170°C (325°F) Gas 3.

Beat the butter, sugar and salt together until smooth. Add the egg yolk and stir until thoroughly combined. Fold in the flour and bring the mixture together to form a smooth dough. Wrap in clingfilm/plastic wrap and leave to rest in a cool place while preparing the filling.

Put the butter, sugar, honey and salt in a saucepan and heat until the sugar has dissolved and the mixture is smooth. Add the cream, let the mixture bubble for 3–4 minutes, then remove from the heat and leave to cool. Stir in the eggs and then the walnuts.

Roll out the pastry on a lightly floured surface and use it to line the tart pan. You will have some left over, but it is impractical to make any less; just freeze any leftovers and use them for something else. Bake the pastry case blind for about 10 minutes, until it is light golden and firm. Leave to cool slightly, then pour the filling evenly over the base. Bake for about 30 minutes, until the filling is golden and set. Serve in slices.

FOR 1 POT OF TEA

3–4 teaspoons tea leaves
sugar or honey, to taste

Warm the pot and add the tea leaves. Pour over boiled, slightly cooled water and leave to brew for 4-5 minutes. Sweeten as desired.

Gunpowder tea is a green tea that dates back to the Tang dynasty of 618–907 AD. It is so named because the leaves are tightly rolled into small balls that were thought to resemble the gunpowder pellets used for cannons, although another theory is that the name comes from the Mandarin term for 'freshly brewed', which is gāng paò dè. Gunpowder tea tends to be quite full flavoured, and is very often used as a base in traditional Moroccan mint tea. Crisp, light pastry wrapping a dark, sticky walnut filling makes this tart one of my favourites (although I admit that I do have a lot of favourites!). I like it served warm, but after a happy accident once, I discovered that when it's refrigerated, the filling turns extra-chewy and delicious, so now that's my little secret treat thing to do with the leftovers.

Russian Caravan Tea
with Crisp Vodka Cookies

Russian Caravan tea is usually created from a blend of Chinese oolong and keemun. The name comes from the 18th-century camel caravans that travelled the ancient trading routes bringing tea from China, Ceylon and India to Russia. The 6,000-mile journey took over 6 months. In modern blends, a little lapsang souchong is added to give a light smoky finish, as it's thought that the camp fires along the journey may have added a slightly smoky flavour to the tea. I'm not sure if the camel drivers themselves would have drunk much of the tea on this lengthy, unforgiving haul, but I'm fairly sure they would have had the odd nip of vodka along the way. So I created these crisp little vodka-laced cookies in their honour. They're probably not terrifically authentic, but delicious all the same.

125 g/1 cup plain/
    all-purpose flour
50 g/½ cup icing/
    confectioners' sugar
a pinch of salt
90 g/6 tablespoons soft
    butter
2 teaspoons vodka
icing/confectioners' sugar,
    for dusting

Makes 12

Preheat the oven to 180°C (350°F) Gas 4.

Put the flour, icing/confectioners' sugar and salt into a large bowl. Rub in the butter until evenly mixed, then add the vodka. Pull the mixture gently but firmly together to form a smooth dough.

Shape the dough into balls the size of walnuts and place on two large non-stick baking sheets, a little distance apart.

Bake for 12–15 minutes until firm and golden. Remove from the oven and transfer to a wire rack to cool. Dust with icing/confectioners' sugar and store in an airtight container.

For 1 Pot of Tea

3-4 teaspoons Russian Caravan tea
milk, to taste
sugar or honey, to taste

Warm the teapot and add the tea leaves and freshly boiled water. Leave to brew for 5 minutes. Add milk and sweeten with sugar or honey, if desired.

375 g/12½ oz. ready-rolled
   puff pastry dough
300 g/1¼ cups good-
   quality cottage cheese
50 g/scant ½ cup ground
   almonds/almond meal
50 g/¼ cup caster/
   superfine sugar
finely grated zest of
   1 lemon
2 egg yolks
25 g/2 tablespoons butter,
   melted
100 g/1 scant cup
   blackcurrants

a 12-cup muffin pan

MAKES 12

ANHUI YELLOW TEA
WITH BLACKCURRANT MAIDS OF HONOUR

*Yellow tea is one of the rarer types of tea and comes from the Anhui,
Sichuan and Hunan provinces in China. Long, slow production gives
it a mellow, sweet flavour and makes it the perfect tea to accompany these
little blackcurrant-speckled tarts. It's important to choose a good-quality
full-fat cheese, full of curds you can get your teeth into – the watery, low-
fat versions will spoil the finished tarts. Remove blackcurrants from their
stems by running them gently through the tines of a fork.*

Preheat the oven to 200°C (400°F) Gas 6.

Roll the dough out on a lightly floured surface. Cut the pastry into
12 rounds and use them to line the muffin pan.

To make the filling, tip the cottage cheese into a bowl and stir
in the almonds, sugar, lemon zest, egg yolks and melted butter. Stir until
everything is well mixed. Fold in the blackcurrants. Spoon the mixture
into the pastry cases. Bake for about 20 minutes, until the filling
is golden and set and the pastry is crisp and brown. Leave
to cool slightly before turning out onto a wire rack to
cool completely.

FOR 1 POT OF TEA
*3-4 teaspoons Anchui yellow tea leaves
boiled but slightly cooled water*

Warm the pot and add the tea
leaves. Boil the water and set aside
to cool for around 5 minutes. Pour
over the cooled water and leave to
brew for about 4 minutes. Sweeten
to taste with sugar or honey.

Earl Grey Tea with Yorkshire Curd Tart

Earl Grey tea is usually produced from a blend of black China tea with bergamot oil. Bergamot is a citrus fruit that looks like a strange cross between an orange and a lime, and is indigenous to Southeast Asia and southern Italy. I'm a Yorkshire gal, and my dad's favourite dish was Yorkshire curd tart. My mum would buy fresh curds, but nowadays it's not easy to find them. I use cottage cheese, which makes a lovely tart, even if not totally authentic. I bet Earl Grey would have loved a slice…

FOR THE PASTRY
175 g/1½ sticks soft butter
50 g/¼ cup caster/
   superfine sugar
1 egg yolk
250 g/2 cups plain/
   all-purpose flour

FOR THE FILLING
500 g/2 cups cottage
   cheese
50 g/scant ½ cup ground
   almonds/almond meal
120 g/⅔ cup caster/
   superfine sugar
a pinch of salt
4 eggs, beaten
100 g/6½ tablespoons
   butter, melted
finely grated zest
   of 2 lemons
100 g/⅔ cup currants
freshly grated nutmeg
icing/confectioners' sugar,
   for dusting

*a 23-cm/9-in fluted tart
   pan with removable base*

SERVES 8-10

To make the pastry, beat the butter and sugar together until light and fluffy. Add the egg yolk and stir until smooth. Add the flour and work the mixture lightly until it forms a soft dough. Wrap the dough in clingfilm/ plastic wrap and leave to rest in a cool place for half an hour, if possible.

Preheat the oven to 180°C (350°F) Gas 4.

Roll out the dough on a lightly floured surface and use it to line the tart pan. There will be some left over, but it will freeze beautifully for another time. Chill the tart case in the freezer while preparing the filling.

Beat the cottage cheese, almonds, sugar, salt and eggs together until smooth. Add the melted butter and lemon zest and beat again. Stir in the currants.

Remove the pastry case from the freezer and bake for about 10 minutes, until biscuit-coloured and firm. Remove from the oven and pour in the filling. Reduce the oven temperature to 150°C (300°F) Gas 2 and bake for about 45 minutes, until the filling has set. Leave to cool in the pan. Dust with icing/confectioners' sugar and serve.

FOR 1 POT OF TEA
*3 teaspoons Earl Grey tea leaves, or use tea bags
sugar or honey, to taste*

Warm the teapot and add the tea leaves. Pour over boiling water. Leave to brew for 5 minutes. Sweeten with sugar or honey, if desired.

ORANGE PEKOE, ORANGE & LEMON PEEL TEA
WITH GLAZED APPLE CAKE

I used to buy a blend of orange pekoe with lemon and orange peels from Bettys Café Tea Rooms in Harrogate, North Yorkshire, the much-loved traditional tea rooms that have gained a national reputation for their amazing teas and pastries. The combination has remained a favourite, so I use oven-dried lemon and orange peels, which I remove with a potato peeler and dry in a very low oven whenever I use the juice and not the zest. Aga owners could use the warming oven.

FOR THE CAKE

150 g/1 stick plus
   2 tablespoons soft butter
150 g/¾ cup caster/
   superfine sugar
2 eggs, beaten
150 g/1⅓ cups ground
   almonds/almond meal
50 g/⅓ cup plain/
   all-purpose flour
finely grated zest of
   2 lemons
1 teaspoon baking powder
100 ml/scant ½ cup milk
2 red apples
5 tablespoons apricot
   jam/jelly

a 20-cm/8-in cake pan with
   removable base, lightly
   greased and lined with
   baking parchment

SERVES 10

Preheat the oven to 160°C (325°F) Gas 3.

Beat the butter and sugar together until light and fluffy. Add the beaten eggs and continue to mix until smooth (you may have to add a little of the flour if the mixture seems to be curdling a little). Add the almonds, flour, lemon zest and baking powder and mix well. Stir in the milk. Spoon the batter into the prepared pan.

Cut the apples in half and remove the core (don't peel them; the skin looks pretty in the finished cake). Cut into thin slices. Starting at the outside edge, arrange the apples in concentric circles, around the cake, slightly overlapping and finishing in the centre.

Bake for about 40 minutes, until the cake is firm and risen and a skewer inserted into the centre comes out clean.

In the meantime, sieve the apricot jam/jelly into a saucepan and add a tablespoon of water.

Remove the cake from the oven and leave to cool for about 15 minutes in the pan. Transfer to a wire rack, brush with the apricot jam/jelly and leave to cool completely.

FOR 1 POT OF TEA

3–4 teaspoons orange pekoe leaves
1 teaspoon each dried lemon and orange peels
sugar or honey, to taste

Warm the teapot and add the tea leaves and citrus peels. Pour over boiling water and leave to brew for 3–4 minutes. Sweeten with sugar or honey, as desired.

ICED LEMON TEA WITH PISTACHIO BROWNIES

Iced tea is normally associated with summer, but it's really nice to keep a jug/pitcher in the fridge all year round because it makes a refreshing cold drink at any time, and with a base of green or white tea, is a healthier alternative to additive-laden fizzy drinks. If you do want a little treat alongside your iced tea, though, these chocolate brownies are dense, delicious and definitely a doddle to make!

250 g/2 sticks butter

500 g/2½ cups caster/
   superfine sugar

100 g/¾ cup cocoa powder

50 g/1½ oz. dark chocolate

4 eggs, beaten

100 g/¾ cup self-
   raising/rising flour

100 g/⅔ cup pistachios,
   roughly chopped

a 20 x 30-cm/8 x 12-in
   roasting pan or cake pan,
   lightly greased

Makes 15

Preheat the oven to 180°C (350°F) Gas 4.

Put the butter, sugar, cocoa powder and dark chocolate in a large heatproof bowl and set it over a saucepan of gently simmering water over low heat, until the butter and chocolate have melted and the sugar has dissolved. Remove from the heat and leave to cool slightly.

Beat in the eggs, and then fold in the flour. Stir in the pistachios.

Spoon the mixture into the prepared pan and bake for about 40 minutes, until firm but still slightly fudgy.

Leave the brownies to cool in the pan, then cut into squares. Store any leftover brownies in an airtight container.

For 1 pot of tea

2–3 green or white tea bags
½ lemon, sliced
sugar or honey, to taste

Put the tea bags in a pot with several lemon slices and pour over boiling water. Leave to infuse for 4–5 minutes. Take out the tea bags and add more lemon slices. Leave to cool, then pour into a jug/pitcher and put in the fridge until ready to use. Serve in tall glasses with ice and extra lemon slices.

ESPRIT DE NOëL TEA
WITH RICH FRUIT CAKE

Drinking a lovely cup of gently spiced tea is a little like enjoying a glass of mulled wine, so a slice of rich fruit cake to eat alongside makes the perfect partnership. A warm mince pie would be heavenly too! The rich fruit cake is almost the same cake I use as my Christmas cake; it's slightly less spiced, so it's a cake you can enjoy all year round.

FOR THE RICH FRUIT CAKE

300 g/2 cups currants

150 g/1 cups raisins

150 g/1 cup sultanas/
  golden raisins

100 g/⅔ cup natural glacé
  cherries, rinsed and
  dried

50 ml/3 tablespoons
  brandy or rum

180 g/1⅓ sticks soft butter

180 g/scant 1 cup soft dark
  brown or molasses sugar

3 eggs, beaten

180 g/1½ cups plain/
  all-purpose flour

1 teaspoon ground
  cinnamon

¼ teaspoon ground
  nutmeg

finely grated zest
  of 1 orange

*a 23-cm/9-in cake pan
  with removable base,
  lightly greased and lined
  with a double layer
  of baking parchment*

SERVES 10

Put the dried fruit and cherries in a large bowl. Pour over the brandy or rum, and leave the mixture to macerate for a few hours, or preferably overnight.

Preheat the oven to 140°C (275°F) Gas 1. Beat the butter and sugar together until it is light and fluffy. Add the eggs, a little at a time, until they are fully incorporated. You may have to add a little flour in between each addition to stop the mixture from curdling. Stir in the remaining flour, spices and orange zest.

Spoon the mixture into the prepared pan. Line the outside of the pan with a double thickness of newspaper and tie it with kitchen string. This will prevent the cake drying out at the edges during the long cooking time. Bake for about 3½–4 hours. Leave to cool in the pan. If you can leave the cake for a week or so, that's great, but you can also eat it straightaway!

FOR 1 POT OF TEA

3-4 teaspoons Esprit de Noel or other Christmas blend tea
sugar and milk, to taste

Warm the teapot and add the tea. Pour over simmering water and let the tea steep for 3–4 minutes. Add milk and sugar as desired.

WHITE DARJEELING TEA
WITH BUTTER-GLAZED LEMON CAKE

White Darjeeling tea is produced from the young leaf buds of tea plants grown in the Darjeeling region of the Himalayas. The leaves are fluffy and light, and for this reason you may find it necessary to use more tea than you would normally expect, so for optimum results it's best to follow the manufacturer's instructions when brewing the tea. The lovely, mellow, slightly sweet tea is absolutely spot-on to slurp with this moist, lemony butter-glazed cake. One cup is never enough for me, and one slice invariably turns into two.

200 g/1¾ sticks soft butter

300 g/2½ cups caster/
superfine sugar

a pinch of salt

3 eggs, beaten

320 g/2½ cups plain/
all-purpose flour

1 teaspoon baking powder

200 ml/¾ cup plain
yoghurt

grated zest of 2 lemons

juice of 1 lemon

FOR THE BUTTER GLAZE

30 g/2 tablespoons butter

a pinch of salt

50 g/¼ cup caster/
superfine sugar

juice of 1 lemon

*a 900-g/2-lb. loaf pan,
lightly greased and lined
with baking parchment*

MAKES AROUND 10 SLICES

Preheat the oven to 180°C (350°F) Gas 4.

Beat the butter, sugar and salt together until light and smooth. Add the beaten eggs a little at a time, until fully incorporated. If the mixture starts to curdle, simply add a little of the flour and stir in.

Add the remaining flour and baking powder, and stir well. Sir in the yoghurt, and then the lemon zest and juice.

Spoon the mixture into the prepared pan and bake for about 1 hour 10 minutes, until golden and risen. A skewer inserted into the centre of the cake should come out clean.

Meanwhile, put the butter, salt, sugar and lemon juice into a small saucepan and heat for 3–4 minutes, until the sugar has dissolved and the mixture is syrupy. Pour over the hot cake.

Leave the cake to cool in the pan for 15 minutes or so, then turn onto a wire rack to cool completely.

FOR 1 POT OF TEA

about 6 teaspoons white Darjeeling tea leaves

Warm the pot and add the tea. Pour over water that has been boiled but cooled very slightly. Leave to infuse for 5 minutes or so before serving.

DINNER PARTY TEAS

Dinner parties don't always have to end with coffee. Matching teas with desserts and after-dinner treats is becoming increasingly popular, and can mean a light and truly luscious end to an evening. With its gentle, lemony flavour, lemon verbena tea makes a great alternative to coffee — add a slice of lemon ricotta tart and you have a fabulous finale to any meal, and that's just one of the mouth-watering combinations that follow.

Korean Yellow Tea with Breton Prune Cake

It's quite a few years since I first tasted traditional Normandy Breton cake filled with sticky prune jam/jelly and fell in love with it, but it remains one of my favourites. If you're not a prune fan, you can substitute other jams/jellies; just make sure they have a high fruit content. Yellow tea has a sweet, mellow flavour that complements the rich cake perfectly.

For the Dough

450 g/3⅔ cups plain/all-purpose flour
300 g/2½ sticks soft butter
225 g/1 cup plus 2 tablespoons caster/
  superfine sugar
6 egg yolks
1 tablespoon rum

For the Filling

450 g/16 oz. good-quality
  prune jam/jelly
1 egg yolk, beaten with
  1 tablespoon milk

*a 23-cm/9-oz. springform
cake pan, lightly greased*

a food processor or stand mixer

Serves 8–10

Preheat the oven to 190°C (375°F) Gas 5.

Place all the dough ingredients in a food processor or mixer and mix until you have a smooth, soft dough. Shape the dough into a ball, wrap in clingfilm/plastic wrap and chill for 1 hour.

Press half the dough into the prepared pan. Spread the jam/jelly over it in an even layer. Carefully cover the jam/jelly with the remaining dough. Brush the dough with the egg glaze and score a diamond pattern in the surface with a sharp knife.

Bake for 15 minutes, then turn the oven down to 180°C (350°F) Gas 4 and bake for a further 40 minutes, until firm and golden.

Leave to cool in the pan, then serve in slices.

For 1 Pot of Tea

*3-4 teaspoons yellow tea leaves   sugar or honey, to taste
boiled, slightly cooled water*

Warm the pot and add the tea leaves. Boil the water and set aside to cool for around 5 minutes. Pour over the cooled water and leave to brew for about 4 minutes. Sweeten to taste with sugar or honey. Milk would spoil this tea.

JASMINE TEA with STICKY RICE CAKE

For many of us, jasmine tea represents our first experience of Chinese tea. Sadly, many commercial jasmine teas are made with low-grade tea, artificially flavoured with jasmine oils or chemically compounded jasmine flavours, and are relatively inexpensive. Try to look for good quality green tea or white tea to which freshly picked jasmine flowers have been added. This sticky rice cake makes a lovely change from traditional flour-based cakes, and is great if you ever need to produce a sweet treat that is gluten-free.

150 g/¾ cup sushi rice

300 ml/1¼ cups coconut
   milk

450 ml/1¾ cups whole
   milk

a pinch of salt

6 kaffir lime leaves

150 g/¾ cup caster/
   superfine sugar

grated zest and juice
   of 1 lemon

3 egg yolks

2 egg whites

a 23-cm/9-in springform
   cake pan, lightly greased

SERVES 15

Put the sushi rice in a saucepan with the coconut milk and whole milk. Stir in the salt, the lime leaves and sugar.

Cook over very gentle heat for about 25 minutes, until the rice is soft. Remove from the heat and leave to cool. Remove the lime leaves.

Preheat the oven to 150°C (300°F) Gas 1.

Stir the lemon zest and juice. Stir in the egg yolks.

Whisk the egg whites to fairly stiff peaks. Fold half the whipped whites into the rice mixture to loosen it, then gently fold in the remaining whites.

Spoon the mixture into the prepared pan and bake for 50 minutes, until set and golden.

FOR 1 POT OF TEA

3–4 teaspoons jasmine tea
sugar or honey, to taste

Warm the pot and add the tea leaves. Pour over boiled, slightly cooled water and leave to brew for 5 minutes. Sweeten with sugar or honey as desired.

Rose Conjou Tea
with Rose Geranium and Muscat Cake

Rose Conjou tea is usually produced from Chinese black tea infused with oil of roses. The black tea leaves are layered several times with rose petals until the natural oils impart the required flavour, creating a really special tea. This glorious dessert cake also takes on the beautiful scent and flavour of roses, imparted by scented geranium leaves (which incidentally are edible). A hefty dousing in gloriously good orange muscat wine makes this cake even more special. End a lovely summer supper with this sublime dessert accompanied by Rose Conjou tea, rather than the more traditional after-dinner coffee.

about 14 small rose-scented geranium leaves

250 g/2 sticks soft butter

250 g/1¼ cups caster/superfine sugar, plus extra for dusting

a pinch of salt

4 eggs, lightly beaten

150 g/1 cup plus 2 tablespoons self-raising/rising flour

100 g/⅔ cup ground almonds/almond meal

50 g/⅓ cup fine polenta or semolina

250–300 ml/1–1¼ cups Brown Brothers Orange Muscat and Flora wine

a 23-cm/9-in springform cake pan, greased, lined with baking parchment and greased again

SERVES 10-12

Preheat the oven to 180°C (350°F) Gas 4.

Carefully arrange the geranium leaves around the outside edge of the prepared pan, close together and with the upper side facing outwards. Set aside.

Beat the butter, sugar and salt together until light and fluffy. Add the eggs a little at a time until fully incorporated. Add the dry ingredients and beat until smooth. Spoon into the prepared pan, taking care not to dislodge the geranium leaves. Bake for about 40 minutes, until golden and springy to the touch.

Remove from the oven and leave to cool for 5 minutes. Pour the muscat wine all over the cake. Leave to cool completely before turning out onto a cake plate. Scatter the top with sugar and serve in slices.

For 1 Pot of Tea
5 teaspoons Rose Conjou tea leaves

Warm the teapot and add the tea leaves. Pour in slightly cooled boiled water and leave to brew for 3–5 minutes. Pour into cups and serve.

SILVER NEEDLE TEA
WITH FRAISES-DES-BOIS FRIANDS

Silver needle white tea has an exquisite sweet, delicate and distinctive flavour and is my very favourite of all teas. It is made from the very tips of the tender, downy buds of tea bushes grown on remote mountainsides in the Fujian Province of south east China. The tips are harvested by hand, for only a few days each year. When you see the tea leaves, they do look like fine, velvety little silver needles. Silver needle tea is high in antioxidants and low in caffeine, so it makes a perfect after dinner drink. I've paired it with moist and moreish friands, made special by the addition of tiny woodland strawberries – a marriage made in heaven I think.

70 g/½ cup ground
  almonds/almond meal

30 g/¼ cup plain/all-
  purpose flour

a pinch of salt

120 g icing/confectioners'
  sugar

100 g/6½ tablespoons
  butter

3 egg whites

80 g/3 oz. fraises des bois

*6 friand moulds,
  lightly greased*

MAKES 6

Preheat the oven to 180°C (350°F) Gas 4.

Mix the almonds, flour, salt and sugar in a large bowl.

Melt the butter in a small saucepan, then remove from the heat and leave to cool. Whisk the egg whites until frothy and light (it's not necessary to whip them into peaks as you would if making meringues).

Trickle the butter into the dry ingredients and add half the egg whites. Mix lightly, and then add the remaining egg whites and continue to mix until they are fully incorporated.

Spoon the mixture into the prepared moulds and scatter the fraises des bois over the top. Bake for about 15 minutes or so, until the friands are risen and golden and spring back when pressed lightly.

Serve warm or leave to cool completely.

FOR 1 POT OF TEA
3–4 teaspoons silver needle white tea

Warm the teapot and add the tea leaves. Pour in boiled and slightly cooled water and leave to brew for 3–4 minutes. Since silver needle tea has such a lovely naturally sweet flavour, do try it first before reaching for the sugar bowl.

FOR THE PASTRY

175 g/1½ sticks soft butter
50 g/¼ cup caster/
  superfine sugar
1 egg yolk
250 g/2 cups plain/
  all-purpose flour

FOR THE FILLING

250 ml/1 cup double/
  heavy cream
500 g/2 cups ricotta
200 g/1 cup caster/
  superfine sugar
3 eggs, beaten
grated zest and juice of
  2 large lemons
icing/confectioners' sugar,
  for dusting

*a 23-cm/9-in fluted tart
  pan with removable base*

SERVES 8

LEMON VERBENA TEA
WITH RICOTTA TART

Lemon verbena tea has a soft lemon flavour that aids digestion, making it a gentle tea to finish a dinner party. It goes exceptionally well with this lovely, light ricotta tart. You can buy tea bags already infused with lemon verbena, but if you have a plant in the garden you can easily infuse the fresh or dried leaves with boiled water – or use a base of green or white tea to up the antioxidant content.

To make the pastry, beat the butter and sugar together until light and fluffy. Add the egg yolk and stir until smooth. Add the flour and work the mixture lightly until it forms a soft dough. Wrap the dough in clingfilm/plastic wrap and leave to rest in a cool place for half an hour.

Preheat the oven to 180°C (350°F) Gas 4. Roll the dough out to fit the tart pan on a lightly floured surface. There will be some left over, but it will freeze beautifully for another time. Chill the tart case in the freezer while preparing the filling.

To make the filling, beat the cream, ricotta, sugar and eggs together until smooth. Add the lemon zest and juice and beat again.

Remove the pastry case from the freezer and bake for about 10 minutes, until biscuit-coloured and firm. Remove from the oven and pour in the filling. Reduce the oven temperature to 150°C (300°F) Gas 2 and bake for about 45 minutes or so, until the filling has set. Leave to cool in the pan. Dust with icing/confectioners' sugar and serve.

FOR 1 POT OF TEA

*3 teaspoons white tea leaves
1 teaspoon dried lemon verbena leaves
sugar or honey, to taste*

Warm the teapot and add the tea leaves and lemon verbena and pour over boiling water. Leave to brew for 5 minutes. Sweeten with sugar or honey.

Lapsang, Souchong, Tea
with Whisky Fruit Tart

Smoky Lapsang Souchong is a little bit of an acquired taste; people either seem to love it or hate it. It's a black tea, from the Fujian province of China, and the smoky flavour and aroma come from the pine fires over which the tea is dried. Good examples of Lapsang Souchong don't have the brash, in your face smell and over-smouldered flavour that cheaper brands do, so if you're going to give this tea a go, do bear that in mind. If you like the thought of a smokey tea now and again, but want a slightly damped-down version, do as I often do, and add just one teaspoonful into a pot of other black tea leaves. A slice of this lovely sticky whisky fruit tart and a cup of smoky tea make a great autumn/fall or winter treat.

FOR THE PASTRY
175 g/1½ sticks soft butter
50 g/¼ cup caster/
   superfine sugar
1 egg yolk
250 g/2 cups plain/
   all-purpose flour, plus
   extra for dusting

FOR THE TOPPING
200 g/1 cup muscovado
   sugar
200 g/1¾ sticks butter
80 ml/⅓ cup whisky
4 eggs, beaten
200 g/1⅓ cups currants
200 g/1⅓ cups raisins
100 g/⅔ cup glacé cherries,
   chopped
150 g/generous 1 cup
   walnuts, chopped
caster/granulated sugar,
   for sprinkling

*a 23-cm/9-in tart pan
   with removable base*

SERVES 8

To make the pastry, cream the butter and sugar together until light and fluffy. Add the egg yolk and beat to combine. Add the flour and bring the mixture together to form a smooth dough. Wrap in clingfilm/plastic wrap and refrigerate for half an hour.

Preheat the oven to 180°C (350°F) Gas 4. Roll the pastry out on a lightly floured surface and line the tart pan with it. You may have some left over, in which case simply freeze it for another time.

To make the topping, put the sugar and butter together in a saucepan and heat until the butter has melted and the sugar has dissolved. Stir in the whisky and leave the mixture to cool a little.

Add the eggs, then stir in the dried fruits and walnuts. Pour the mixture over the pastry base and bake for 30 minutes, or until the topping has set. Sprinkle with caster sugar and leave to cool. Serve in slices.

FOR 1 POT OF TEA
3–4 teaspoons Lapsang Souchong tea leaves
sugar or honey, to taste
milk, to taste

Warm the pot and add the tea leaves. Pour over boiling water and leave to brew for 3–5 minutes. Add sugar or honey and milk, as desired.

FOR THE PASTRY
175 g/1½ sticks soft butter
50 g/¼ cup caster/
   superfine sugar
1 egg yolk
250 g/2 cups plain/
   all-purpose flour

FOR THE FILLING
2 egg yolks
2 whole eggs
300 ml/1¼ cups double/
   heavy cream
50 g/¼ cup caster/
   superfine sugar
3 tablespoons elderflower
   cordial
200 g/1⅓ cups
   gooseberries, topped
   and tailed

eight 5-cm/2-in tartlet pans
   with removable base

MAKES 8

GINGER AND HONEY TEA
WITH GOOSEBERRY CUSTARD TARTLETS

Ginger fans will love this tea – there's enough flavour from the ginger to create a zingy, refreshing drink without actually adding tea leaves in any form, but you may prefer the additional depth a little green tea adds. Served with creamy gooseberry and elderflower custard encased in crisp pastry makes a pretty terrific twosome.

For the pastry, cream the butter and sugar together until light and fluffy. Stir in the egg yolk until fully combined. Lightly fold in the flour until the mixture forms a soft, smooth dough. Roll the mixture out to a thickness of about 2 mm (⅛ in) and cut out 8 rounds about 6 cm (2½ in) diameter. Line the tartlet pans, taking care to press the mixture into the corners. Refrigerate for 30 minutes.

Preheat the oven to 180°C (350°F) Gas 4. Beat the egg yolks, whole eggs and cream together until smooth. Stir in the sugar and elderflower cordial. Remove the tartlet pans from the fridge and set them on a baking sheet. Scatter a few gooseberries evenly across the base of each one and divide the custard mixture between them, spooning the mixture carefully over the gooseberries. Bake for about 25 minutes, until the filling is set and golden. Leave to cool, turn out of the pans and serve.

FOR 1 POT OF TEA
4 green tea bags, or the equivalent in tea leaves
5 cm/2 in fresh ginger root, sliced
a light, flowery honey, such as acacia honey, to taste

Warm the teapot and add the green tea and ginger. Fill the teapot with boiling water. Give everything a gentle stir and leave to infuse for 4–5 minutes. Sweeten to taste and pour into cups.

Formosa Oolong Tea
with Fig and Mascarpone Tart

Formosa oolong tea is grown and produced in Taiwan. With its distinctive appearance, taste and aroma, it has earned a place among the world's finest teas. Oolong tea is also alleged to have many far-reaching health benefits. It is believed by many to help aid weight loss too – the caffeine in it supposedly speeds up the metabolism and helps burn extra calories (which is lucky, because that means you can tuck into a slice of this dreamy fig-laden tart without the tiniest trace of guilt).

For the Pastry
175 g/1½ sticks soft butter
50 g/¼ cup caster/
   superfine sugar
a pinch of salt
1 egg yolk
250 g/2 cups plain/all-
   purpose flour

For the Filling
50 g/1½ oz. white
   chocolate, melted
250 g/1 cup mascarpone
18–20 fresh, ripe figs
6 tablespoons apricot
   jam/jelly, strained

a 20-cm/8-in tart pan
   with removable base

Serves 6–8

Preheat the oven to 180°C (350°F) Gas 4.

Beat the butter, sugar and salt together until smooth. Add the egg yolk and stir until thoroughly combined. Fold in the flour and bring the mixture together to form a smooth dough. Wrap in clingfilm/plastic wrap and leave to rest in a cool place for 30 minutes.

Roll out the pastry and use it to line the tart pan. There will be some pastry left over, but you can freeze the leftovers and use them for something else. Bake the pastry case blind for about 10 minutes or so, until light golden and firm. Leave to cool.

Brush the base of the tart with melted white chocolate and leave it to set. In the meantime, beat the mascarpone gently for a minute or two, until smooth and light. Spoon the mascarpone into the tart and spread it out in an even layer.

Quarter the figs and arrange them vertically in the mascarpone, working in concentric circles and placing them close together, until the pastry case is full and there are no gaps.

Place the jam/jelly in a small saucepan and add 1 tablespoon water. Stir until smooth and gently brush the figs to give them a nice shiny glaze.

For 1 Pot of Tea
8 teaspoons Formosa oolong (Ti Kuan Yin is sublime)

Warm the teapot and add the tea leaves. Boil the kettle and allow the water to cool slightly. Pour the water over the leaves and leave to infuse for 4–10 minutes, to taste.

Japanese Cherry Tea
with Raspberry Ripple Cheesecakes

Sakura is a cherry tree indigenous to Japan and is in blossom from late March to May. Sencha green tea leaves combined with the dried flowers of the Sakura cherry is a well-loved tea, and rightly so. Le Palais des Thés make a lovely cherry tea called Fleur de Geisha; the smell is heavenly and the tea is addictive – an amazing accompaniment to these lovely, light sponge-bottomed cheesecakes.

For the bases
60 g/4 tablespoons soft
  butter
120 g/⅔ cup caster/
  granulated sugar
2 eggs, beaten
60 g/½ cup self-raising/
  rising flour
2 lemons

For the topping
250 g/1 cup mascarpone
250 g/8 oz. full-fat cream
  cheese
70 g/⅓ cup caster/
  granulated sugar
250 g/2 cups raspberries

To decorate
200 g/1½ cups redcurrants
150 g/1 cup raspberries
caster/granulated sugar,
  for dusting

*a 23-cm/9-in cake pan,
  lightly greased and lined
  with baking parchment*

6 deep, plain cookie cutters

Makes 6

Preheat the oven to 180°C (350°F) Gas 4.

To make the bases, beat the butter and half the sugar together until light and fluffy, then stir in the eggs a little at a time until fully incorporated. Add the flour and beat until smooth. Spoon the mixture into the prepared pan and level gently with a palette knife. Bake for 10 minutes or so, until golden, risen and springy.

Meanwhile, grate the zest from the lemons into a large bowl and set it aside for the filling. Squeeze the juice from the lemons into a separate bowl and stir in the remaining sugar. Spoon this over the freshly baked sponge as soon as it has been removed from the oven. Set aside.

For the topping, mix the mascarpone and cream cheese in the same bowl as the lemon zest. Add 50 g/¼ cup of the sugar and beat until the mixture is very smooth and fluffy.

Push half of the raspberries for the filling through a fine sieve set over a bowl and stir in the remaining 20 g/2 tablespoons sugar. Fold in the remaining raspberries, crushing them very lightly with a fork, just to break them up slightly. Fold them gently through the mascarpone to create a lightly rippled effect. Chill the mixture for a couple of hours to firm up. Don't be tempted to skip the chilling time for the cheese mixture, as it needs time to firm up.

Cut 6 circles out of the sponge with the cookie cutters or rings. Set the rings on pretty serving plates and place a sponge circle in the base of each one. Spoon in enough cheese mixture to come to the top. Top each cheesecake with a stem of redcurrants and a few raspberries. Chill until ready to eat. Just before serving, carefully remove the metal rings and dress with fresh berries.

FOR 1 POT OF TEA

2–4 teaspoons Japanese cherry tea leaves
boiled but slightly cooled water

Warm the teapot and add the tea leaves.
Add the boiled but slightly cooled water
and leave to brew for 3 minutes.

Pi Lo Chun Tea
with white chocolate, cardamom and ginger cheesecake

Pi Lo Chun is a Chinese green tea picked in early spring from the valleys and slopes of Taiwan. Pi Lo Chun means 'Spring Green Snail' and was named so by the Emperor Kang Xi because he thought the steeped leaves looked just like tiny snails. The bushes are co-planted with apricot, plum and peach trees, and the leaves absorb some of the scent, giving them a characteristic aroma and fruity, fragrant taste. I've paired this special tea with an equally special treat – a divine cheesecake that never fails to please.

For the base
100 g/½ cup caster/
  granulated sugar
100 g/⅔ cup ground
  almonds/almond meal
100 g/¾ cup plain/all-
  purpose flour
100 g/6½ tablespoons
  butter, melted

For the topping
200 ml/¾ cup double/
  heavy cream
3–4 green cardamom pods
750 g/24 oz. cream cheese
100 g/½ cup caster/
  granulated sugar
6 eggs plus 3 egg yolks
250 g/8 oz. white chocolate
100 g/3½ oz. stem ginger,
  finely chopped
icing/confectioners' sugar,
  for dusting

*a 23-cm/9-in springform
cake pan, lightly greased
and lined with baking
parchment*

Serves 12–15

Preheat the oven to 180°C (350°F) Gas 4.

Put the sugar, almonds and flour into a bowl. Add the melted butter and stir until well mixed. Press the mixture into the prepared pan and bake for about 10 minutes, until firm and golden. Remove and set aside.

Reduce the oven temperature to 140°C (275°F) Gas 1. Pour the cream into a small saucepan. Bash the cardamom pods with a rolling pin and add the pods and black seeds to the pan. Bring to the boil, then turn off the heat and leave to infuse.

In the meantime, beat the cream cheese, sugar, eggs, and egg yolks together until smooth. Sieve the cream into a clean pan and reheat gently until almost simmering. Remove from the heat, then add 200 g/6½ oz. of the white chocolate and stir until melted. Leave to cool, then beat into the cheese mixture. Scatter the stem ginger over the cheesecake base and pour the cheese mixture slowly over it, trying not to dislodge the ginger.

Bake for about 1½ hours, until set. Turn off the oven and leave it to cool with the door very slightly ajar. Once cool, transfer to the fridge. To decorate, melt the remaining white chocolate and drizzle it in a zig-zag pattern across the top. Dust with icing/confectioners' sugar and serve.

For 1 pot of tea
*3–4 teaspoons Pi Lo Chun tea leaves
sugar or honey, to taste*

Warm the pot and add the leaves. Pour over boiled and slightly cooled water and leave to brew for 2–3 minutes. Sweeten with sugar or honey, as desired.

INDEX

SOURCES

UK
Bettys Café Tea Rooms
1 Parliament Street
Harrogate HG1 2QU
+44 (0)1423 814 070
www.bettys.co.uk

Cafedirect
24 Great King Street
Edinburgh EH3 6QN
www.cafedirect.co.uk

JING Teas
Canterbury Court
London SW9 6DE
+44 (0)20 7183 2113
www.jingtea.com

The Tea House
15 Neal Street, Covent Garden
London WC2H 9PU
+44 (0)20 7240 7539
www.theteahouseltd.com

Whittard of Chelsea
Windrush House
Windrush Park Road
Witney OX29 7DX
+44 (0) 1993 893 715
www.whittard.co.uk

US
Adagio Teas
617 N State Street
Chicago IL 60654
www.adagio.com

Culinary Teas
61 Cudworth Lane
Sudbury MA 01776
(1)-866-799-4005
www.culinaryteas.com

Harney & Sons Fine Teas
433 Broome Street
New York NY 10013
(1)-888-427-6398
www.harney.com

Teas Etc
480 Tall Pines Rd, Suite C
West Palm Beach FL 33413
(1)-800-832-1126
www.teasetc.com

BUSINESS CREDITS

Ryland Peters & Small would like to thank The Tea House (Covent Garden) and JING Tea for providing materials for the photography in this book.